OH SAY CAN YOU SEE

THE UNMENTIONED HISTORY OF TERRORISM ON BLACKS IN AMERICA

STORY TOLD AND WRITTEN BY

FRANK ZAAQAN JORDAN

The Unmentioned History Of Terrorism On Blacks In America

Story told and written by

Frank Zaaqan Jordan

Oh Say Can You See...

The Unmentioned History Of Terrorism On Blacks In America

Story told and written by Frank Zaaqan Jordan

First Edition- Printing November 2020

Zaaqan1212@yahoo.com

ISBN#- 9798557835251

Oh Say Can You See

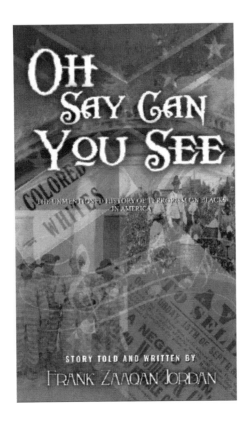

The Unmentioned History Of Terrorism On Blacks In
America

Story told and written by

Frank Zaaqan Jordan

Introduction

The American education system has consistently built and fabricated the unmentioned history of Blacks, Latinos, and the Natives. But what they fail to mention as it pertains to how the American government foundation was truly built.

American history intentionally eradicates the deceptive, evil manner in which the European explorers not only manipulated the Natives out of this great land which is now called the United States of America, but real history proves thousands if not millions of Black slaves, along with the natives were savagely murdered under normal circumstances by Europeans.

The United States still to this day maintains the practices of unlawfully stealing land that rightfully doesn't belong to them as a government, these historical events are hardly if not mentioned at all in the curriculum of the education system.

This history book is written to open your eyes, and awaken your soul to a spiritual level of intelligence society has hidden for centuries.

"And that knowing the time, it is high time to awake out of sleep"

Romans 13:11

All praises to the great and mighty Yahawah wa Yahawahshi

Contents

Chapter One

Terrorism Explained

Terrorism,

The calculated use of unlawful violence or threat of unlawful violence to in calculate fear; intended to coerce or to intimidate governments or societies in pursuit of goals that are generally political, religious, or ideological; the act of terrorizing; the state of being terrorized.

(*Ref; US Dept. of Defense, Random House Kernerman Webster's College Dictionary 2010 k Dictionaries ltd*.)

The US undoubtedly has had a consistent history and pattern of demonstrated terrorism throughout its course of history. Starting from voyages of the explorations of Christopher Columbus in the late 1400's, to the modern-day intentional terrorism leveled across the globe by modern day world leaders, governments, scientist, and European presidents. These acts of deviate, inhumane thoughts are frequently questioned but never answered entirely. Without question blacks in America have come across severe acts of unkindness from European Caucasians deliberately and most assumingly calculated.

To the misfortune of African Americans here in the United States one can argue that the same treatments are equal across the board, but history, statistics, and factual evidence show and proves quite differently. Blacks have never been treated or looked upon by most white Americans as equal, but socially disadvantaged to ever amass the identical amount of wealth or afforded opportunities as Caucasians. Some may say or disagree with the modern day choices of education systems that are available to Blacks and Hispanics to partake as a way of being or having a fair chance to become a professional worker in America. In addition to obtaining the lure of material wealth, better education, social justice, civil rights, along with your local state law enforcers.

Contrary to belief during the Atlantic Slave Trade, (*or Euro- American slave trade involved the transportation by European-Caucasian, Arab, French, The British, along with The Spanish(Spain; Spaniards) enslaved Blacks, Negroes mainly to the Americas, and throughout the Caribbean Islands. The slave trade regularly used the triangle trade route as its middle passage, and existed from the 16th to the 19th centuries*).

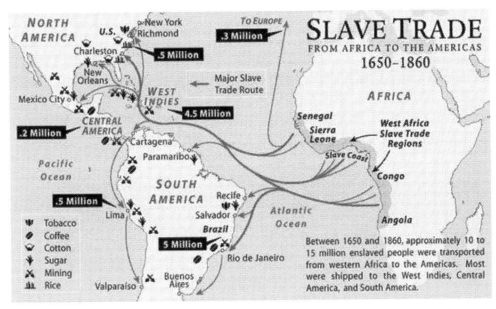

The Atlantic Slave Trade lasted between 1600's-1800's which involved the selling of more than 15 million Black negroe slaves.

<u>*Treatment of Slaves;*</u>

At no given time in history during the Atlantic slave trade given the research, documented letters written by European ship masters, and crewmen there isn't any evidence whereas Black slaves enroute to the Americas, Europe and the Islands of the Caribbean they were treated with the red carpet rolled out, in fact nothing can be further from the truth. In fact slaves once captured and unwillingly forced on board these European slave ships were underfed and treated brutally causing many to die before arriving at their destinations; dead or dying slaves were dumped overboard for shark feed. They were not treated as human, living like animals throughout their long voyage to the New World.

Slave ships spent several months travelling to different parts of the coast, buying their cargo. The captives were often in poor health from the physical and mental abuse they had suffered. They were taken on board, stripped naked and examined from head to toe by the captain or surgeon.

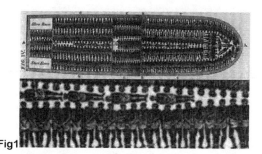
Fig1

Conditions on board ship during the Middle Passage were appalling. The men were packed together below deck and were secured by leg irons. The space was so cramped they were forced to crouch or lie down. Women and children were kept in separate quarters, sometimes on deck, allowing them limited freedom of movement, but this also exposed them to violence and sexual abuse from the crew.(fig1.)

The air in the hold was foul and putrid. Seasickness was common and the heat was oppressive. The lack of sanitation and suffocating conditions meant there was a constant threat of disease. Epidemics of fever, dysentery (the 'flux') and smallpox were frequent. Captives endured these conditions for about two months, sometimes longer.

In good weather the captives were brought on deck in midmorning and forced to exercise. They were fed twice a day and those refusing to eat were force-fed. Those who died were thrown overboard.

The combination of disease, inadequate food, rebellion and punishment took a heavy toll on captives and crew alike. Surviving records suggest that until the 1750s one in five Africans on board ship died.

Some European governments, such as the British and French, introduced laws to control conditions on board. They reduced the numbers of people allowed on board and required a surgeon to be carried. The principal reason for taking action was concern for the crew and not the captives.

The surgeons, though often unqualified, were paid head-money to keep captives alive. By about 1800 records show that the number of Africans who died had declined to about one in eighteen.

(*Eyewitness to history* ;)

In 1807 the British Parliament passed a bill prohibiting the slave trade. In January the following year the United States followed suit by outlawing the importation of slaves. The acts did nothing to curtail the trade of slaves within the nation's borders, but did end the overseas commerce in slaves. To enforce these laws, Britain and the United States jointly patrolled the seas off the coast of Africa, stopping suspected slave traders and confiscating the ship when slaves were found. The human cargo was then transported back to Africa.

Interception at Sea

Conditions aboard the slave ships were wretched. Men, women and children crammed into every available space, denied adequate room, food or breathing space. The stench was appalling - the atmosphere inhumane to say the least. The Reverend Robert Walsh served aboard one of the ships assigned to intercept the slavers off the African coast. On the morning of May 22, 1829, a suspected slaver was sighted and the naval vessel gave chase. The next day, a favorable wind allowed the interceptor to gain on its quarry and approach close enough to fire two shots across her bow. The slaver heaved to and an armed party from the interceptor scrambled aboard her. We join Reverend Walsh's account as he boards the slave ship:

"The first object that struck us was an enormous gun, turning on a swivel, on deck - the constant appendage of a pirate; and the next were large kettles for cooking, on the bows - the usual apparatus of

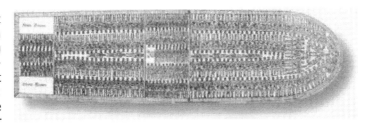

Plan for "stowage" of a slaveship, 1790

a slaver. Our boat was now hoisted out, and I went on board with the officers. When we mounted her decks we found her full of slaves. She was called the *Feloz*, commanded by Captain Jose' Barbosa, bound to Bahia. She was a very broad-decked ship, with a mainmast, schooner rigged, and behind her foremast was that large, formidable gun, which turned on a broad circle of iron, on deck, and which enabled her to act as a pirate if her slaving speculation failed. She had taken in, on the coast of Africa, 336 males and 226 females, making in all 562, and had been out seventeen days, during which she had thrown overboard 55. The slaves were all inclosed under grated hatchways between decks. The space was so low that they sat between each other's legs and [were] stowed so close together that there was no possibility of their lying down or at all changing their position by night or day. As they belonged to and were shipped on account of different individuals, they were all branded like sheep with the owner's marks of different forms. These were impressed under their breasts or on their arms, and, as the mate informed me with perfect indifference 'burnt with the red-hot iron.' Over the hatchway stood a ferocious-looking fellow with a scourge of many twisted thongs in his hand, who was the slave driver of the ship, and whenever he heard the slightest noise below, he shook it over them and seemed eager to exercise it. I was quite pleased to take this hateful badge out of his hand, and I have kept it ever since as a horrid memorial of reality, should I ever be disposed to forget the scene I witnessed.

As soon as the poor creatures saw us looking down at them, their dark and melancholy visages brightened up. They perceived some- thing of sympathy and kindness in our looks which they had not been accustomed to, and, feeling instinctively that we were friends, they immediately began to shout and clap their hands. One or two had picked up a few Portuguese words, and cried out, "Viva! Viva!" The women were particularly excited. They all held up their arms, and when we bent down and shook hands with them, they could not contain their delight; they endeavored to scramble up on their knees, stretching up to kiss our hands, and we understood that they knew we were come to liberate them. Some, however, hung down their heads in apparently hopeless dejection; some were greatly emaciated, and some, particularly children, seemed dying.

But the circumstance which struck us most forcibly was how it was possible for such a number of human beings to exist, packed up and wedged together as tight as they could cram, in low cells three feet high, the greater part of which, except that immediately under the grated hatchways, was shut out from light or air, and this when the thermometer, exposed to the open sky, was standing in the shade, on our deck, at 89'. The space between decks was divided into two compartments 3 feet 3 inches high; the size of one was 16 feet by 18 and of the other 40 by 21; into the first were crammed the women and girls, into the second the men and boys: 226 fellow creatures were thus thrust into one space 288 feet square and 336 into another space 800 feet square, giving to the whole an average Of 23 inches and to each of the women not more than 13 inches. We also found manacles and fetters of different kinds, but it appears that they had all been taken off before we boarded.

The heat of these horrid places was so great and the odor so offensive that it was quite impossible to enter them, even had there been room. They were measured as above when the slaves had left them. The officers insisted that the poor suffering

Cross section of the stowage of a slave ship, 1790

creatures should be admitted on deck to get air and water. This was opposed by the mate of the slaver, who, from a feeling that they deserved it, declared they would murder them all. The officers, however, persisted, and the poor beings were all turned up together. It is impossible to conceive the effect of this eruption - 517 fellow creatures of all ages and sexes, some children, some adults, some old men and women, all in a state of total nudity, scrambling out together to taste the luxury of a little fresh air and water. They came swarming up like bees from the aperture of a hive till the whole deck was crowded to suffocation front stem to stern, so that it was impossible to imagine where they could all have come from or how they could have been stowed away. On looking into the places where they had been crammed, there were found some children next the sides of the ship, in the places most remote from light and air; they were lying nearly in a torpid state after the rest had turned out. The little creatures seemed indifferent as to life or death, and when they were carried on deck, many of them could not stand.

After enjoying for a short time the unusual luxury of air, some water was brought; it was then that the extent of their sufferings was exposed in a fearful manner. They all rushed like maniacs towards it. No entreaties or threats or blows could restrain them; they shrieked and struggled and fought with one another for a drop of this precious liquid, as if they grew rabid at the sight of it.

It was not surprising that they should have endured much sickness and loss of life in their short passage. They had sailed from the coast of Africa on the 7th of May and had been out but seventeen days, and they had thrown overboard no less than fifty-five, who had died of dysentery and other complaints in that space of time, though they had left the coast in good health. Indeed, many of the survivors were seen lying about the decks in the last stage of emaciation and in a state of filth and misery not to be looked at. Even-handed justice had visited the effects of this unholy traffic on the crew who were engaged in it. Eight or nine had died, and at that moment six were in hammocks on board, in different stages of fever. This mortality did not arise from want of medicine. There was a large stock ostentatiously displayed in the cabin, with a manuscript book containing directions as to the quantities; but the only medical man on board to prescribe it was a black, who was as ignorant as his patients.

Image from an abolitionist
pamphlet, 1837

While expressing my horror at what I saw and exclaiming against the state of this vessel for conveying human beings, I was informed by my friends, who had passed so long a time on the coast of Africa and visited so many ships, that this was one of the best they had seen. The height sometimes between decks was only eighteen inches, so that the unfortunate beings could not turn round or even on their sides, the elevation being less than the breadth of their shoulders; and here they are usually chained to the decks by the neck and legs. In such a place the sense of misery and suffocation is so great that the Negroes, like the English in the Black Hole at Calcutta, are driven to a frenzy. They had on one occasion taken a slave vessel in the river Bonny; the slaves were stowed in the narrow space between decks and chained together. They heard a horrible din and tumult among them and could not imagine from what cause it proceeded. They opened the hatches and turned them up on deck. They were manacled together in twos and threes. Their horror may be well conceived when they found a number of them in different stages of suffocation; many of them were foaming at the mouth and in the last agonies-many were dead. A living man was sometimes dragged up, and his companion was a dead body; sometimes of the three attached to the same chain, one was dying and another dead. The tumult they had heard was the frenzy of those suffocating wretches in the last stage of fury and desperation, struggling to extricate themselves. When they were all dragged up, nineteen were irrecoverably dead. Many destroyed one another in the hopes of procuring room to breathe; men strangled those next them, and women drove nails into each other's brains. Many unfortunate creatures on other occasions took the first opportunity of leaping overboard and getting rid, in this way, of an intolerable life."

References:
Walsh, Robert, Notices of Brazil in 1828 and 1829 (1831).

How To Cite This Article:
"Aboard a Slave Ship, 1829," EyeWitness to History, www.eyewitnesstohistory.com (2000).

On board slave ships often times sick, disobedient, or dead slaves were thrown overboard to be fed to the man-eating sharks during the Trans-Atlantic Slave Trade.

The Transatlantic slave trade is known as the largest involuntary forced migration in the history of the world. Sharks migratory patterns were changed because these predators followed the ships in the Middle Passage because when a slave died they were thrown overboard, or they were killed because they were rebelling or committed suicide, the sharks knew that they could follow the ships, and it changed the migratory patterns of sharks during this period of time.

History suggests that during the Atlantic Slave Trade (1500-1869), more than 15.5 million Black slaves with documented statistics show about 1.8 million of them dying along the way, that's a rate of about 15percent. In addition many African Americans died before ever making it to the ships, and another 15 percent died soon after their arrival.

The *Zong Massacre;*

The Zong massacre was the mass killing of more than 130 enslaved Black negroes by the crew of British slave ship Zong on and in the days following 29 November 1781. The

Gregson slave-trading syndicate, based in Liverpool, owned the ship and sailed her in the Atlantic slave trade. As was common business practice, they had taken out insurance on the lives of the enslaved people as cargo. According to the crew, when the ship ran low on drinking water following navigational mistakes, the crew was ordered to throw the slaves overboard into the sea.

Famous painting of 1840 by J.M.W Turner shown above Black Slaves being thrown overboard and being fed to the sharks below in the sea.

<u>Rep. John Lewis, (D-GA</u>), once quoted as saying" sharks still follow ships across the Atlantic today, looking for people that have been thrown overboard", referring bto the slave vessels long ago.

Inhumane buying and selling of Blacks on auction blocks

Upon the arrival to America Negroe slaves were treated in such a reckless intentional manner from White Europeans it's hardly any wonder any survived the sufferings at the hands of the slave owners. From the very egregious journey here it took an average of one to two months to complete the journey. Enslaved Blacks were naked and shackled together with several different types of chains (iron), stored like cattle on the floor beneath bunks with little to no room to move due to the cramped conditions. European slave traders left very little room aboard these cargo ships for men, women and children every inch of space they used to cram Black slaves was used with very little breathing space, and very little food.

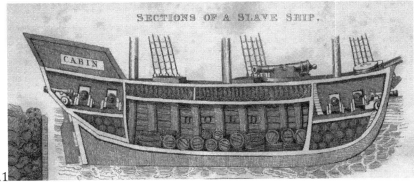

Fig.1

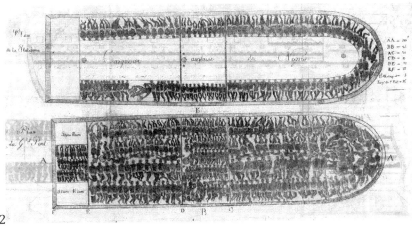

Fig.2

Fig 1. (Previous page),

Rev. Robert Walsh records the condition of the enslaved Blacks on Board the Feloz(1829)

Rev. Robert Walsh (1772–1852) was a clergyman, physician and writer who hailed from Co. Waterford. He was a son of a wealthy merchant family and he studied at Trinity College Dublin from 1789 to 1796. During this time he befriended the Irish patriot-to-be Robert Emmet and the poet Thomas Moore. Ordained in 1802, he became the curate of Finglas in 1806. He accepted the offer of chaplaincy to the British embassy in Constantinople in 1820, but became ill during his voyage there and was quarantined in Belgrade. He was next stationed in Saint Petersburg before being offered the chaplaincy to the embassy in Rio de Janeiro in 1828. This is where Walsh enters our narrative. His description of the chattel slave system in Brazil is damning. In his view the traders at one slave mart handled their victims "exactly as I have seen butchers feeling a calf." Returning to England in 1829, the frigate on which Walsh was a passenger spotted a slave ship and began to pursue it. His account of the condition of the enslaved people (and its immensely depressing conclusion) is both memorable and invaluable.

When we mounted her decks we found her full of slaves. She was called the *Feloz*, commanded by Captain Jose Barbosa, bound to Bahia. She was a very broad-decked ship, with a mainmast, schooner rigged, and behind her foremast was that large, formidable gun, which turned on a broad circle of iron, on deck, and which enabled her to act as a pirate if her slaving speculation failed. She had taken in, on the coast of Africa, 336 males and 226 females, making in all 562, and had been out seventeen days, during which she had thrown overboard 55.

"The slaves were all enclosed under grated hatchways between decks. The space was so low that they sat between each other's legs and were stowed so close together that there was no possibility of their lying down or at all changing their position by night or day."

Illustration from Walsh's 'Notices', p. 478

"As they belonged to and were shipped on account of different individuals, they were all branded like sheep with the owner's marks of different forms. These were impressed under their breasts or on their arms, and, as the mate informed me with perfect indifference "burnt with the red-hot iron."

Illustration of slave brandings from Walsh's 'Notices', p. 479

Over the hatchway stood a ferocious-looking fellow with a scourge of many twisted thongs in his hand, who was the slave driver of the ship, and whenever he heard the slightest noise below, he shook it over them and seemed eager to exercise it. I was quite pleased to take this hateful badge out of his hand, and I have kept it ever since as a horrid memorial of reality, should I ever be disposed to forget the scene I witnessed.

As soon as the poor creatures saw us looking down at them, their dark and melancholy visages brightened up. They perceived something of sympathy and kindness in our looks which they had not been accustomed to, and, feeling instinctively that we were friends, they immediately began to shout and clap their hands. One or two had picked up a few Portuguese words, and cried out, *"Viva! Viva!"* The women were particularly excited. They all held up their arms, and when we bent down and shook hands with them, they could not contain their delight; they endeavored to scramble up on their knees, stretching up to kiss our hands, and we understood that they knew we were come to liberate them.

"Some, however, hung down their heads in apparently hopeless dejection; some were greatly emaciated, and some, particularly children, seemed dying."

But the circumstance which struck us most forcibly was how it was possible for such a

number of human beings to exist, packed up and wedged together as tight as they could

cram, in low cells three feet high, the greater part of which, except that immediately

under the grated hatchways, was shut out from light or air, and this when the

thermometer, exposed to the open sky, was standing in the shade, on our deck, at 89'.

The space between decks was divided into two compartments 3 feet 3 inches high; the

size of one was 16 feet by 18 and of the other 40 by 21; into the first were crammed the

women and girls, into the second the men and boys: 226 fellow creatures were thus

thrust into one space 288 feet square and 336 into another space 800 feet square, giving

to the whole an average Of 23 inches and to each of the women not more than 13 inches.

We also found manacles and fetters of different kinds, but it appears that they had all

been taken off before we boarded.

The heat of these horrid places was so great and the odour so offensive that it was quite

impossible to enter them, even had there been room. They were measured as above when

the slaves had left them.

"The officers insisted that the poor suffering creatures should be admitted

on deck to get air and water. This was opposed by the mate of the slaver,

who, from a feeling that they deserved it, declared they would murder

them all."

The officers, however, persisted, and the poor beings were all turned up together. It is impossible to conceive the effect of this eruption — 517 fellow creatures of all ages and sexes, some children, some adults, some old men and women, all in a state of total nudity, scrambling out together to taste the luxury of a little fresh air and water. They came swarming up like bees from the aperture of a hive till the whole deck was crowded to suffocation front stem to stern, so that it was impossible to imagine where they could all have come from or how they could have been stowed away. On looking into the places where they had been crammed, there were found some children next the sides of the ship, in the places most remote from light and air; they were lying nearly in a torpid state after the rest had turned out.

"The little creatures seemed indifferent as to life or death, and when they were carried on deck, many of them could not stand."

After enjoying for a short time the unusual luxury of air, some water was brought; it was then that the extent of their sufferings was exposed in a fearful manner. They all rushed like maniacs towards it. No entreaties or threats or blows could restrain them; they shrieked and struggled and fought with one another for a drop of this precious liquid, as if they grew rabid at the sight of it. It was not surprising that they should have endured much sickness and loss of life in their short passage.

"They had sailed from the coast of Africa on the 7th of May and had been out but seventeen days, and they had thrown overboard no less than fifty-five..."

...who had died of dysentery and other complaints in that space of time, though they had left the coast in good health. Indeed, many of the survivors were seen lying about the decks in the last stage of emaciation and in a state of filth and misery not to be looked at. Even-handed justice had visited the effects of this unholy traffic on the crew who were engaged in it. Eight or nine had died, and at that moment six were in hammocks on board, in different stages of fever. This mortality did not arise from want of medicine. There was a large stock ostentatiously displayed in the cabin, with a manuscript book containing directions as to the quantities; but the only medical man on board to prescribe it was a black, who was as ignorant as his patients.

"While expressing my horror at what I saw and exclaiming against the state of this vessel for conveying human beings, I was informed by my friends, who had passed so long a time on the coast of Africa and visited so many ships, that this was one of the best they had seen."

The height sometimes between decks was only eighteen inches, so that the unfortunate beings could not turn round or even on their sides, the elevation being less than the breadth of their shoulders; and here they are usually chained to the decks by the neck and legs.

In such a place the sense of misery and suffocation is so great that the Negroes, like the English in the Black Hole at Calcutta, are driven to a frenzy. They had on one occasion taken a slave vessel in the river Bonny; the slaves were stowed in the narrow space between decks and chained together. They heard a horrible din and tumult among them and could not imagine from what cause it proceeded. They opened the hatches and turned them up on deck. They were manacled together in twos and threes. Their horror may be well conceived when they found a number of them in different stages of suffocation; many of them were foaming at the mouth and in the last agonies-many were dead. A living man was sometimes dragged up, and his companion was a dead body; sometimes of the three attached to the same chain, one was dying and another dead.

The tumult they had heard was the frenzy of those suffocating wretches in the last stage of fury and desperation, struggling to extricate themselves. When they were all dragged up, nineteen were irrecoverably dead. Many destroyed one another in the hopes of procuring room to breathe; men strangled those next them, and women drove nails into each other's brains.

"Many unfortunate creatures on other occasions took the first opportunity of leaping overboard and getting rid, in this way, of an intolerable life. "But due to the conditions of the *Treaty of Brazil* the enslavers were allowed to proceed with their "cargo". Walsh's final description of the slave ship continuing on its way is absolutely devastating.

the limits of legal traffic. It was with infinite regret, therefore, we were obliged to restore his papers to the captain, and permit him to proceed, after nine hours' detention and close investigation. It was dark when we separated, and the last parting sounds we heard from the unhallowed ship, were the cries and shrieks of the slaves, suffering under some bodily infliction.

Punishment on board slave ship 1792

(*Reference; Rev Robert Walshs notices of Brazil in 1828 and 1829, pages 472-494)*

Black Slave Auctions in America;

During the Trans-Atlantic which lasted from the 16th-19th century not only was one of the most grueling barbaric terroristic acts known to mankind, but upon the arrival of these slave ships during the centuries of slave trading. The Slaves were met at the shores of the Americas with the most cruel and unusual punishments from the traders, Caucasian merchants, auctioneers and land owners. Black men, women and children as young as 2-3years old were shuffled off the ships and prepared for what would prove to be one of the most prophetic moments in the history of this entire universe. Black Slaves (Israelites) to be sold over a course of over three centuries on auction blocks into captivity and slavery.

"And the Lord shall bring thee into Egypt again with ships, by the way I spake unto thee, thou shalt see it no more again, and there ye shall be sold unto your enemies for bondmen and bond women...... Deuteronomy 28:68"

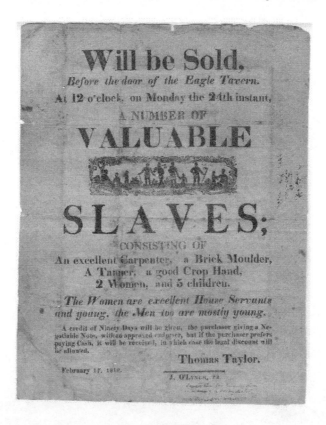

February 17th 1812, S.C Black men, women and young children slaves were sold during the pinnacle of the slave trade.

1857

55 PRIME NEGROES,

Accustomed to the culture of Rice.

By LOUIS D. DeSAUSSURE.

On Wednesday, 21st January, 1857, at

will be sold in families, at 11 o'clock, A. M., in the city of Charleston,

An uncommonly prime gang of Rice-Field Negroes.

CONDITIONS :—One-third Cash. Balance by Bond, payable in two equal annual Installments, with interest, payable annually from day of sale, to be secured by a mortgage of the property, and approved personal security. Purchasers to pay for papers.

Nos.		Ages	
1	John	50	trusty driver, full hand.
2	Mary	40	prime
3	June	20	"
4	Paddy	16	3-4 hand, cart boy
5	Lydia	9	
6	Love	6	
7	Charity	2	
8	Ben	60	1-2 hand
9	Patty	60	"
10	George	30	prime
11	July	28	"
12	Jacob	26	"
13	Bacchus	25	"
14	Flanders	23	"
15	Patience	30	full hand & house serv't
16	Clarinda	14	house girl
17	Infant	5 months	
18	Guy	35	prime hand, deaf
19	Hannah	35	" trusty
20	Harriet	15	3-4 prime girl
21	Cretia	7	
22	Joshua	2	
23	Binah	20	prime
24	Abram	1	
25	Cyrus	22	prime
26	Plymouth	19	"
27	Nanny	35	full hand
28	Bess	7	
29	Scilla	30	full hand, recently had dysentery.
30	Taggy	40	3-4 hand
31	Juba	50	1-2 hand, plantation cook
32	Tenah	22	prime
33	Infant	6 months	
34	Jenny	20	prime
35	Manwell	1	
36	Moses	23	prime
37	Paul	35	prime, trunk minder
38	Jacob	45	full hand, ploughman and wagoner.
39	Manwell	55	1-2 jobbing carpenter
40	Dorcas	40	3-4 child's nurse
41	Penda	4	
42	Rinah	20	prime
43	May	2	
44	London	50	full hand, complains.
45	Martha	23	prime
46	Jack	19	full hand, ploughman
47	Solomon	16	3-4 "
48	Andrew	13	1-4 hand
49	Pompey	30	full hand, one eye
50	Dianah	28	3-4 hand
51	Maggy	5	
52	Adam	55	3-4 hand
53	Maria	50	1-2 hand, sick nurse, sickly
54	Mary	20	prime
55	Ned	4	

Black Negroe Slaves sold Weds January 21st 1857, Charleston, S.C, as advertised in this ad.

Price, Birch & Co, Slave Black Slave dealers, Alexandria, Virginia location 1315 Duke street, *(photo courtesy of Library of Congress)*

Price, Birch& Co

Fig 1.

(Fig.1)The original owners were Franklin & Armfield "Dealers In Slaves" which was known to be the largest dealers in black slaves in the nation during the 1820's to 1830's, this firm is said to have shipped more than 1000-1200 slaves per year to New Orleans, LA, and Natchez, Mississippi.(top)

The holding cell of slaves, Price, Birch & Co. 1820's (photo courtesy of Library of Congress)

(Slave auction blocks cont.);

1864

1864 Whitehall street, Atlanta, GA "Auction and Negro Sales" (above)

The remains of an actually slave auction block, located on the corner of William and Charles streets
Fredericksburg, VA from (1850)

Old Slave auction Block

Old Slave Block, Fredericksburg, Virginia

Fredericksburg, Virginia a postcard photo (above) of the actual corner of William and Charles Street where Black Slaves were auctioned off to white slave masters

An actual flyer promoting the sale of slaves, Fredericksburg, VA 1800's

Another actual slave auction block located at Warrington, VA

A PRIME GANG OF 158 NEGROES.

By LOUIS D. DeSAUSSURE.

On Tuesday, the 13th March, 1860, at 11 o'clock, A. M.,

WILL BE SOLD IN

CHARLESTON, S. C., AT THE MART IN CHALMERS ST.

BY ORDER OF

The Executors of the late T. Bennett Lucas,

A REMARKABLE GANG OF

158 NEGROES,

ACCUSTOMED TO WORKING IN A RICE MILL,

MANY OF WHOM HAVE BEEN PLANTATION NEGROES. ABOUT NINETY
ARE MEN, AMONG WHOM ARE COOPERS, BLACKSMITHS, ENGINEERS,
CARPENTER, AND VALUABLE HOUSE SERVANTS. &c.

CONDITIONS.—One-third cash, the balance by Bonds, bearing legal interest, payable in two
equal annual instalments, (to be arranged by the Executors in sums to suit the liquidation of
the debts of the Estate,) to be secured by a mortgage of the Negroes, and approved personal
security. Purchasers to pay for all requisite papers.

WALKER, EVANS & CO., PRINTERS, 3 BROAD STREET.

(Slave auction blocks cont.);

This Black Slave auction block still remains located at Main and Court streets in Luray, VA at the chamber of Commerce building.

The written testimony stands next to the Slave Auction Block located in Luray, VA

Fig.1

The Green Hill Plantation, located state route 728 Campbell County Virginia, (pic courtesy of library of Congress)

fig.2

The Green hill Plantation still has the actual black slave auction block were they were auctioned off and sold, men, women, and children

Slave Auction, 1859

Printer Friendly Version >>>

In early March 1859 an enormous slave action took place at the Race Course three miles outside Savannah, Georgia. Four hundred thirty-six slaves were to be put on the auction block including men, women, children and infants. Word of the sale had spread through the South for weeks, drawing potential buyers from North and South Carolina, Virginia, Georgia, Alabama and Louisiana. All of Savannah's available hotel rooms and any other lodging spaces were quickly appropriated by

the influx of visitors. In the days running up to the auction, daily excursions were made from the city to the Race Course to inspect, evaluate and determine an appropriate bid for the human merchandise on display.

The sale's magnitude was the result of the break-up of an old family estate that included two plantations. The majority of the slaves had never been sold before. Most had spent their entire lives on one of the two

Announcing a Slave Auction, 1829

plantations included in the sale. The rules of the auction stipulated that the slaves would be sold as "families" - defined as a husband and wife and any offspring. However, there was no guarantee that this rule would be adhered to in all cases.

The sale gained such renown that it attracted the attention of Horace Greeley, Editor of the *New York Tribune*, one of America's most influential newspapers at the time. Greeley was an abolitionist and staunchly opposed to slavery. He sent a reporter to cover the auction in order to reveal to his readers the barbarity inherent in one human being's ability to own and sell another.

Preparation...

"The slaves remained at the race-course, some of them for more than a week and all of them for four days before the sale. They were brought in thus early that buyers who desired to inspect them might enjoy that privilege, although none of them were sold at private sale. For these preliminary days their shed was constantly visited by speculators. The negroes were examined with as little consideration as if they had been brutes indeed; the buyers pulling their mouths open to see their teeth, pinching their limbs to find how muscular they were, walking them up and down to detect any signs of lameness, making them stoop and bend in different ways that they might be certain there was no concealed rupture or wound; and in addition to all this treatment, asking them scores of questions relative to their qualifications and accomplishments.

All these humiliations were submitted to without a murmur and in some instances with good-natured cheerfulness - where the slave liked the appearance of the proposed buyer, and fancied that he might prove a kind 'mas'r.'

The following curiously sad scene is the type of a score of others that were there enacted:

'Elisha,' chattel No. 5 in the catalogue, had taken a fancy to a benevolent looking middle-aged gentleman, who was inspecting the stock, and thus used his powers of persuasion to induce the benevolent man to purchase him, with his wife, boy and girl, Molly, Israel and Sevanda, chattels Nos. 6, 7 and 8. The earnestness with which the poor fellow pressed his suit, knowing, as he did, that perhaps the happiness of his whole life depended on his success, was interesting, and the arguments he used were most pathetic. He made no appeal to the feelings of the buyer; he rested no hope on his charity and kindness, but only strove to show how well worth his dollars were the bone and blood he was entreating him to buy.

'Look at me, Mas'r; am prime rice planter; sho' you won't find a better man den me; no better on de whole plantation; not a bit old yet; do mo' work den ever; do carpenter work, too, little; better buy me, Mas'r; I'se be good sarvant, Mas'r. Molly, too, my wife, Sa, fus rate rice hand; mos as good as me. Stan' out yer, Molly, and let the gen'lm'n see.'

Molly advances, with her hands crossed on her bosom, and makes a quick short curtsy, and stands mute, looking appealingly in the benevolent man's face. But Elisha talks all the faster.

'Show mas'r yer arm Molly - good arm dat mas'r - she do a heap of work mo' with dat arm yet. Let good mas'r see yer teeth Molly - see dat mas'r, teeth all reg'lar, all good - she'm young gal yet. Come out yer Israel, walk aroun' an' let the gen'lm'n see how spry you be.'

Then, pointing to the three-year-old girl who stood with her chubby hand to her mouth, holding on to her mother's dress, and uncertain what to make of the strange scene.

'Little Vardy's on'y a chile yet; make prime gal by-and-by. Better buy us mas'r, we'm fus' rate bargain" - and so on. But the benevolent gentleman found where he could drive a closer bargain, and so bought somebody else..."

The Sale...

"The buyers, who were present to the number of about two hundred, clustered around the platform; while the Negroes, who were not likely to be immediately wanted, gathered into sad groups in the background to watch the progress of the selling in which they were so sorrowfully interested. The wind howled outside, and through the open side of the building the driving rain came pouring in; the bar down stairs ceased for a short time its brisk trade; the buyers lit fresh cigars, got ready their catalogues and pencils, and the first lot of human chattels are led upon the stand, not by a white man, but by a sleek mulatto, himself a slave, and who seems to regard the selling of his brethren, in which he so glibly assists, as a capital joke. It had been announced that the Negroes would be sold in "families," that is to say; a man would not be parted from his wife, or a mother from a very young child. There is perhaps as much policy as humanity in this arrangement, for thereby many aged and unserviceable people are disposed of, who otherwise would not find a ready sale...

...The expression on the faces of all who stepped on the block was always the same, and told of more anguish than it is in the power of words to express. Blighted homes, crushed hopes and broken hearts was (sic) the sad story to be read in all the anxious faces. Some of them regarded the sale with perfect indifference, never making a motion save to turn from one side to the other at the word of the dapper Mr. Bryan, that all the crowd might have a fair view of their proportions, and then, when the sale was accomplished, stepping down from the block without caring to cast even a look at the buyer, who now held all their happiness in

his hands. Others, again, strained their eyes with eager glances from one buyer to another as the bidding went on, trying with earnest attention to follow the rapid voice of the auctioneer. Sometimes, two persons only would be bidding for the same chattel, all the others having resigned the contest, and then the poor creature on the block, conceiving an instantaneous preference for one of the buyers over the other, would regard the rivalry with the intensest (sic) interest, the expression of his face changing with every bid, settling

On the Block
From a Contemporary Illustration

into a half smile of joy if the favorite buyer persevered unto the end and secured the property, and settling down into a look of hopeless despair if the other won the victory...

The auctioneer brought up Joshua's Molly and family. He announced that Molly insisted that she was lame in her left foot, and perversely would walk lame, although, for his part, he did not believe a word of it. He had caused her to be examined by an eminent physician in Savannah, which medical light had declared that Joshua's Molly was not lame, but was only shamming. However, the gentlemen must judge for themselves and bid accordingly. So Molly was put through her paces, and compelled to trot up and down along the stage, to go up and down the steps, and to exercise her feet in various ways, but always with the same result, the left foot would be lame. She was finally sold for $695. [equivalent to approximately $15,300 in today's dollars]

Whether she really was lame or not, no one knows but herself, but it must be remembered that to a slave a lameness, or anything that decreases his market value, is a thing to be rejoiced over. A man in the prime of life, worth $1,600 [equivalent to approximately $35,200 in today's dollars] or thereabouts, can have little hope of ever being able, by any little savings of his own, to purchase his liberty. But, let him have a rupture, or lose a limb, or sustain any other injury that renders him of much less service to his owner, and reduces his value to $300 or $400, and he may hope to accumulate that sum, and eventually to purchase his liberty. Freedom without health is infinitely sweeter than health without freedom.

And so the Great Sale went on for two long days, during which time there were sold 429 men, women and children. There were 436 announced to be sold, but a few were detained on the plantations by sickness...

The total amount of the sale foots up $303,850." [equivalent to approximately $6,700,000 in today's dollars]

References:
    New York Daily Tribune, March 9, 1859 reprinted in Hart, Albert B., American History Told by Contemporaries v. 4 (1928).

Fig.1

Charlottesville, VA the caption reads "Slave Auction Block, On This Site Slaves Were Bought and Sold" (fig.1)

Fig.2

The old Slave Mart Museum located at 6 Chalmers St, Charleston, S.C, Possibly the only known building used as a slave auction site in South Carolina from 1856-1863 still in existence today. In Charleston, enslaved Blacks were customarily sold in the open area north of the Old Exchange building at Broad and East Bay Streets.(fig 2)

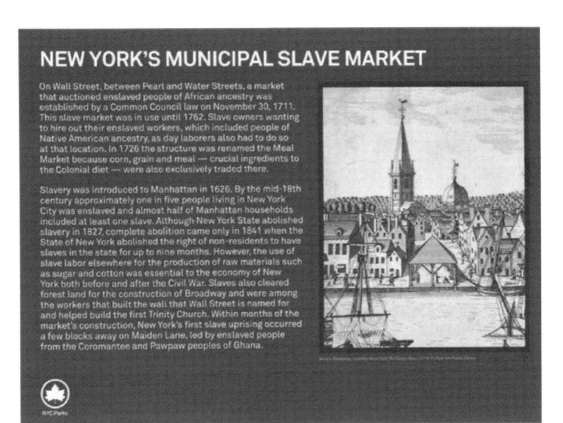

"On Wall Street, between Pearl and Water streets, a market that auctioned enslaved people of African American ancestry was established by a Common Council law on November 30, 1711. This slave market was in use until 1762. Slave owners wanting to hire out their enslaved workers, which included people of Native American ancestry, as day laborers also had to do so at that location. In 1726 the structure was renamed the Meal Market because corn, grain and meal crucial ingredients to the Colonial diet, were also exclusively traded there"..........(top half of writing, ref NYC Parks)

Wall Street, New York City

Records of Slave Trading in New York City *(credit New York historical Society)*

Black slave burial ground, Wall Street, Lower Manhattan, NYC

NEW YORK — Wall Street and much of this city's renowned financial district were built on the burial ground of African slaves, and New York's prosperity stems in large part from the grotesque profits of the African slave trade and African enslavement.

This is the inescapable conclusion one draws from the evidence presented in a major exhibition on "Slavery in New York," which opened here Oct. 7 and runs through March 26. Hosted by the New-York Historical Society, the exhibition is the most impressive display ever mounted on slavery in the Empire State and in New York City in particular.

The exhibition features public programs, walking tours, educational materials and programs for school, college and adult learners. It explores the vital role that slave trading, the labor of enslaved people, and slavery's integration with everyday commerce played from 1600 to 1827 in making New York the wealthiest city in the world.

Hidden history

For a phenomenon that should be common knowledge, the role of New York in the Atlantic slave trade is buried deep in the underground of U.S. history and outside of the consciousness of many New Yorkers. Each year thousands of students in the nation's largest school system study the history of New York with hardly a mention of this city's experience with slavery.

Granted, slavery in America has traditionally been identified primarily as southern experience. Yet there were more enslaved Africans in New York before the American Revolution than any other city except Charleston, S.C.

During this period, 1 out of every 5 New Yorkers was enslaved. At one point, 40 percent of colonial New York's households owned slaves.

To the millions of multi-generational Caribbean immigrants residing in the greater New York area, the exhibition displays should also reflect a slavery Diaspora that is not often recognized as incorporating the Caribbean and New York in very intimate ways.

Many of New York's enslaved had originated from the Caribbean. Banishment from the American colonies (the US after independence) to the harsher conditions of the sugar cane plantations of the West Indies was a constant threat to rambunctious Africans. And New York corporate interests financed much of the slave trade in the Caribbean. There are several portraits at the exhibition that make this connection by depicting conditions of Caribbean slavery.

In his book "The Atlantic Slave Trade: A Census", Philip D. Curtin reminds us that between 1715 - 67 New York and New Jersey imported the vast majority of its 4,551 slaves directly from the West Indies [Curtin 1969: 143].

And a colonial musical chair ultimately resulting in the treaty of Versailles (1783) - in which Britain gains Dominica, Grenada, St Vincent and Tobago - was duly noted as a significant juncture in the New York slavery timeline.

Dr Eric Williams

It is with these interconnections in mind, as well as a sense of the intrinsic value of history to future generations, that Trinidad and Tobago's founder, Dr. Eric Eustace Williams (1911-1981), dedicated his 1963 "Documents of West Indian History" to "the young people of the West Indies as an aid in their struggle against the legacy, the mentality and the fragmentation of colonialism" [Williams 1963].

William's most well known work "Capitalism and Slavery" remains one of the seminal research projects on slavery and the inter-relationship of these phenomena. Focusing on the English-speaking Caribbean, Williams argued that Britain's 'triangular trade' provided a critical foundation for the industrial revolution.

Though not negating the significant role played by slave abolitionists, Williams posited that chattel slavery was abolished principally because that mode of production was no longer necessary for the further development of capitalism. By tracing the development of capitalist industrialization up the red rivers of African slavery, Williams' thesis was critical not only for an understanding on the dialectics of capitalism and slavery, but to the function of institutional racism as a by-product of slavery, an ideology that sought to justify slavery. "Slavery was not born of racism; rather, racism was the consequence of slavery." [Williams 1944: 129]

A jolting discovery

But it was the discovery of the African Burial Ground in the heart of New York's financial district in 1991 that put the spotlight on the seemingly forgotten dark underbelly of U.S. and global capitalism – the literal African slavery skeletons in its closets. The huge, 18th-century burial ground uncovered during painstaking excavations — following the abortive construction of a skyscraper on the site — eventually revealed the remains of some 419 Africans, a large proportion of them women and children.

At that time the city consisted of the southern tip of Manhattan, stretching up to where today's City Hall exists. The burial ground extends from Broadway, southward under City Hall, and touches almost to the site of the former World Trade Center, in close proximity to Wall Street's financial center.

The African cemeteries in the Wall Street area were buried long ago when surrounding hills were flattened and deposited there as foundation for buildings that now serve as a major nerve center of the world economy. It is believed that there are as many as 20,000 slavery-era Africans in graves under the constellation of buildings in lower Manhattan.

Manhattan Island had a population of enslaved Africans almost from the very beginning of settlement in 1624. The findings of scientists examining the graves show that enslaved Africans lived agonizing lives. They were overworked and underfed. Many died young. The average life expectancy of Africans of that era was 37 years.

Slavery's global reach

The largest forced migration in world history, the Atlantic slave trade involved an estimated 40,000 ships, carrying an average of 80 persons a day for more than 400 years. The astounding profits from this trade fueled the industrial revolution in England and later in Europe and the United States.

New York's strategic, geographical position, its proximity to other American colonial settlements, as well as its network of inland waterways, made it a prime center for the slave trade and the accumulation of capital from very early on. The Empire City was an important nexus in a far-flung web commanded by the Dutch East India Company. That web involved a base in Angola on Africa's Atlantic shore, a base in Brazil South America, and one in Curaçao in the Dutch Caribbean.

The first slaves arrived in what was then known as New Amsterdam around 1627. These enslaved Africans worked for the Dutch West India Company rather than for individuals. In addition to building the wall that gives Wall Street its name — a wall of timber and earthwork along the northern boundary of New Amsterdam — slaves cleared Manhattan's forests, turned up the soil for farming, built roads and constructed buildings. Without slave labor New Amsterdam might not have survived.

As a rule, unlike the slaves of the South, New York slaves did not live in quarters with large numbers of other Black people, but in kitchens or back rooms of their owners' houses. Many white New Yorkers owned one or two slaves.

(ref; Black In America, The Social Network For Socially Conscious African Americans)

Lehman Brothers, NYC

Cotton from a bale sold at the New York Cotton Exchange, which Southern merchants like the Lehman Brothers made into the leading cotton futures market, 1875

The cotton economy of the nineteenth century, accounting by most measures for more than half of the total goods exported from the US between 1820 and 1860, helped form many of America's current economic and social institutions: the carceral system, property laws, and insurance industry, modern finance systems— all have roots in the Southern slave economy. The profits created by the cotton business helped fund vast empires of trade and industry, including shipping and railroads. They also enriched middlemen: insurers, brokers, investors, and speculators, which is where the Lehmans enter the story. The American economy of the 1820s and 1830s was undergoing a transformation thanks to the development of new debt instruments secured by the use of slaves as collateral. The value of chattel slaves could be transferred into mortgages, securities, and bonds, like any other financial asset that could then be sold to investors nationally and internationally.(*Ref:The New York Review of Books, "The Lehman Trilogy" and Wall street Debt to Slavery*)

Black Slavery;

"A nation of fierce countenance, which shall not regard the person of the old, nor shew favor to the young" (Deuteronomy 28:50)

During the late 1500's- 1800's Black negroes were carted and shipped to the shores of the United States auctioned, sold to European slave owners throughout the U.S on various plantation farms. Upon arriving to these plantations not only were the young children sold off like cattle, but also suffered the most unimaginable treatment leveled against them. Most children were sold into slavery specifically to serve as male harlots (Bucks) for slave breeding, and young girls were forced against their will to serve as slaves and also raped continually. Most were threatened with their lives had this been mentioned, most Black female slaves in most cases would rather commit suicide before being raped by Europeans.

1860

The Slave Manifest of the S.S. Texas from La Salle to New Orleans arrived March 5, 1860(ref; U.S National Archives)

(Black slavery cont.);

1864

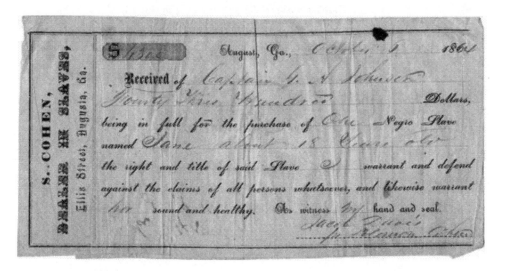

A purchase receipt of buying a black slave. "Dealer in Slaves Augusta, GA 1864, Purchase of one Negroe slave, $1,300"

Late 1800's Negroe Slaves men, women and children, Augusta GA.

How Black women resisted slave breeding by using cotton roots as contraceptives.

Young female slaves picking cotton

The couple of years following the prohibition of slave importation into the US was an era of slave farming. After 1808, slave labor was a scarce commodity in the United States. It was a period that heralded the collapse of a highly lucrative business where the stock traded were humans whose lives were as perishable as autumn leaves. But the slave owners were good businessmen. They knew that no business survives with borders closed on supplies. These slavepreneurs did what every good business man would do, they found an alternative means of supply – slave breeding. Slave breeding was a slave multiplication agenda. It was implemented by slave owners through a forced sexual relation between the male and female slaves and between masters and their female slaves. This sexual relation was solely intended to result in pregnancies to reproduce slave children as essential stock for trade. The motive was entirely profit-oriented. The slave owners ensured that where force didn't work, they encouraged this procreation by favoring the female slaves who had more children. In some cases, freedom was promised to those who could produce as much as fifteen slave children.

A Black woman and her large family

Notably, slave breeding bypassed the experimental level and went straight to a highly structured business strategy. Slave girls were expected to start reproducing from the age of thirteen and should have five children at least by the age of twenty.

Meanwhile, the slaves who managed to escape before the American civil war, testified to their experience in books that became the literary genre known as the slave narratives. These books recorded stories of slaves forced into marriages and compelled into sexual relations with their male counterparts. They recorded the sexual abuse of female slaves by their masters and overseers.

A good example is the testimony of Maggie Stenhouse, an ex-slave. In her words, "Durin' slavery there were stockmen. They was weighed and tested. A man would rent the stockman and put him in a room with some young women he wanted to raise children from."

A black woman with her mulatto children

Slave breeding should have been an ingenious investment idea if the livestock reared and harvested weren't humans. But it didn't matter to the slavepreneurs how their business decisions affected this group of humans, especially as they have been named slaves. However, it always matters when your livestock have minds of their own, and can choose to use it against you.

A slave family working on a cotton plantation

Consequently, black women began to think for themselves more cleverly than their masters. They picked up the courage to frustrate the attempt to be used as involuntary surrogates. They knew better than to continue birthing children that were snatched from their breasts sooner than they could breathe on their own. They knew it was suicidal to confront their masters directly, but they also knew that not all pregnancies must be born.

Accordingly, these women perfected the science of <u>contraception</u> with the use of herbs to prevent or <u>terminate pregnancies</u>. They spread the popular conspiracy amongst themselves that chewing on cotton roots wipes the womb clean of any germinating life. Scientists found that the cotton plant contains a poisonous pigment known as gossypol. It is believed that this substance has the ability to restrict the mobility of sperm and alter the menstrual cycle by preventing the secretion of certain hormones.

Chewing cotton roots as a contraceptive or to induce abortion was common among slave women that labored in cotton fields. Other less popular abortifacient included the peacock flower. Women who couldn't lay hold of the cotton roots made use of the peacock flower to achieve the same aim of frustrating the idea of slave breeding.

Slave women were forced against their will to have relations with European slave owners

Black Male Buck Breaking, Breeding Farms

FLOGGING A SLAVE FASTENED TO THE GROUND.

The Making of African American Identity: Vol. I, 1500-1865 For many enslaved African Americans, one of the cruelest hardships they endured was sexual abuse by the slaveholders, overseers, and other white men and women whose power to dominate them was complete. Enslaved women were forced to submit to their masters' sexual advances, perhaps bearing children who would engender the rage of a master's wife, and from whom they might be separated forever as a result. Masters forcibly paired "good breeders" to produce strong children they could sell at a high price. Resistance brought severe punishment, often death. "I know these facts will seem too awful to relate," warns former slave William J. Anderson in his 1857 narrative, ". . . as they are some of the real 'dark deeds of American Slavery.'" „ On Slaveholders' Sexual Abuse of Slaves „ Selections from 19th- & 20th-century Slave Narratives Presented here are selections from two groups of narratives: 19th-century memoirs of fugitive slaves, often published by abolitionist societies, and the 20th-century interviews of former slaves compiled in the 1930s by the Works Progress Administration (WPA) Slave Narrative Project (reproduced here as transcribed by the interviewers).1* 1 Plenty of the colored women have children by the white men. She know better than to not do what he say. Didn't have much of that until the men from South Carolina come up here [North Carolina] and settle and bring slaves. Then they take them very same children what have they own blood and make slaves out of them. If the Missus find out she raise revolution. But she hardly find out. The white men not going to tell and the nigger women were always afraid to. So they jes go on hopin' that thing[s] won't be that way always. W. L. BOST, enslaved in North Carolina, interviewed 1937 [WPA Slave Narrative Project] „ The slave traders would buy young and able farm men and well developed young girls with fine physique to barter and sell. They would bring them to the taverns where there would be the buyers and traders, display them and offer them for sale. At one of these gatherings a colored girl, a mulatto of fine stature and good looks, was put on sale. She was of high spirits and determined disposition. At night she was taken by the trader to his room to satisfy his bestial nature. She could not be coerced or forced, so she was attacked by him. In the struggle she grabbed a knife and with it, she sterilized him and from the result of injury he died the next day. She was charged with murder. Gen. Butler, hearing of it, sent troops to Charles County [Maryland] to protect her, they brought her to to Baltimore, later she was taken to Washington where she was set free. . . This attack was the result of being goodlooking, for which many a poor girl in Charles County paid the price. There are several cases I could mention, but they are distasteful to me. . . .

These male slaves were purchase based entirely on the prerequisite of them possessing a large penis. Black men were routinely raped by their gay slave owners. The process was known as "breaking the buck."

Black male slave breeding farms were a normal site during the 16th-18th century

Slave Branding

BRANDING A NEGRESS AT THE RIO PONGO
From a wood engraving in Canot's *Twenty Years of an African Slaver,*
New York, 1854

Among the most potent weapons in the rhetorical arsenal of abolitionism was the charge that slaves were physically mutilated by branding, "like sheep or cattle" author <u>Thomas Clarkson</u> (1760–1846), an ignominious "mark of property," which served to debase enslaved people and split them off from the humanity of the master class (1788, p. 124). In (Macaulay 1824, p. 73). This was, according to recent decades, however, historians have taken little notice of branding, either with regard to its prevalence, purposes, or impact upon bondpeople.In the early twentieth century, even conservative scholars such as Ulrich Phillips (1877–1934) and Charles Sydnor (b. 1898) admitted that "negroes were sometimes branded on the chest or face," though their research in newspapers and plantation and legal records argued that, by the antebellum period, such treatment was reserved for those considered as slave criminals—runaways, thieves, and recalcitrants (Sydnor 1933, p. 89). Under English law, branding was applied most commonly as punishment for theft or flight by indentured servants and apprentices from the Elizabethan period onward, and colonial and state governments in <u>the South</u> carried the practice down to secession on whites and blacks alike. In <u>South Carolina</u>, for example, branding robbers in the hand, or marking fugitives with the letter R (for runaway) went hand in hand in the legal code from 1690 with such other barbarities as slitting noses and carving off ears. By the early nineteenth century, however, branding as a punishment for crime largely fell into disuse, not least because of the widespread adoption of whipping as an educative mechanism of social discipline. For historians searching out the origins of paternalist slave management strategies, this shift seems crucial.

Originally, however, branding seems to have served a commercial purpose on the African coast. It marked blacks as the living property of another, and conferred upon them an ineradicable identity with their owner. In 1744, geographer Joseph Randal reported that merchants engaged in the Guinea slave trade marked their purchases with hot irons to distinguish them from one another prior to making the <u>Middle Passage</u>. Because the human chattels of various traders were lumped together in coastal pens and on shipboard, branding allowed for easy sorting as well as commodification. Two generations later, <u>Samuel Hopkins</u> (1721–1803) described the practice as universal. "All that are passed as fit for sale," he noted "are branded with a hot iron in some part of their body, with the buyer's mark" (1785, p. 14)

Branding Irons used on Slaves

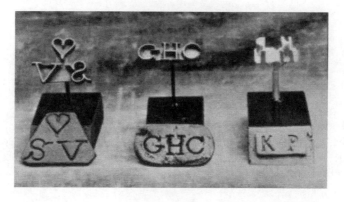

AMERICAN SLAVE BRANDING IRON, GEORGIA PLANTATION

Item Date:

ca. 1750 - 1850

Object name(s):

iron

Catalog ID:

-

Tags: branding, Georgia Plantation, Slavery

Description:

18th and 19th Century (circa 1750 – 1850) American Slave Branding Iron, Georgia plantation. Captured and kidnapped from usually Africa, American slaves were branded once at their site of departure to show ownership as the slaves would mix while being transported to their site of sale, with this brand, specifically America. When they were sold, they would be branded with the new owner's brand, and this would repeat with each resale. Specific slave owners like to brand in specific visible places, i.e. the forehead, the cheek, or the upper arm.

Branding irons used on Slaves during the 1600's-1800

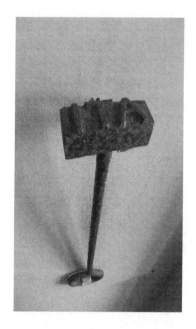

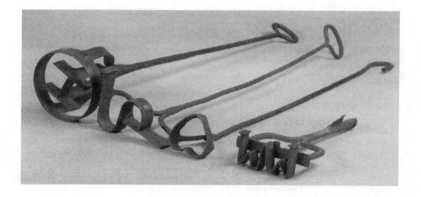

Chapter Two

Free Slave Labor

Fortune 500 Companies that have benefited from free slave labor

Once black slaves set foot upon the American soil not only were they systematically sold off to various slave owners and numerous plantations mostly throughout the southern regions of the U.S. because of the rich soil that would allow superb farming and great agriculture produce that would in turn regenerate the beginning of an enormous amount of generational wealth for White Americans, but even moreso the black slaves received no pay or less to no wages for their hard labor throughout America for over more than 400 years. Not only didn't the Caucasian slave owners along with the American government didn't compensate the slaves for their hard dreadful labor, but in fact most of the white American Fortune 500 companies that are now standing today, were founded off the hard labor, and the backs of Black slavery. From the early 1600's to the late 1800's America has benefited in more ways imaginable from black slavery, and still to this very day the U.S. has yet to consider or entertain the thought of "*reparations*" to each family of slave descendants.

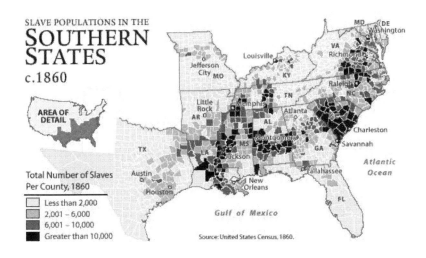

United States map of slavery in the Southern Regions during 1860

John Charles Fremont

John Charles Fremont 1856 a candidate for the new Republican Party is shown here opposite a map that shows the areas of the U.S. of Free states and slave states, as shown most slave states(heavy black ink) were located in the Southern regions of the U.S.(*ref; Adolphus Greely, life of Charles Fremont, Greely &McElrath, New York 1856*)

1800's

The enslavement of African people in the Americas by the nations and peoples of Western Europe, created the economic engine that funded modern capitalism. Therefore it comes as no surprise that most of the major corporations that were founded by Western European and American merchants prior to roughly 100 years ago, benefited directly from slavery.

1800's

(Free slave labor cont.);

Aetna Health Life Insurance

Aetna Insurance Company organized an annuity fund to sell life insurance in 1850. In 1853 the annuity Department separates from Aetna Insurance and incorporated as Aetna life Insurance Company. The name "Aetna" was inspired by an 11,000 foot volcano on the eastern shores of Sicily, Mt Etna.

Aetna, Inc., the United States' largest health insurer, apologized for selling policies in the 1850s that reimbursed slave owners for financial losses when the enslaved Africans they owned died.

"Aetna has long acknowledged that for several years shortly after its founding in 1853 that the company may have insured the lives of slaves," said Aetna spokesman Fred Laberge in 2002. "We express our deep regret over any participation at all in this deplorable practice."

(Ref; Atlanta Black Star)

(Free Slave labor cont);

J.P Morgan inc

John Piepont Morgan Sr, was an American financier and banker who dominated corporate finance on Wall Street throughout the Gilded Age. As the head of the banking firm that ultimately became known as J.P Morgan & Co. He was a driving force behind the wave of industrial consolidation in the United States spanning the late 19th and 20th centuries.

JPMorgan Chase admitted their company's links to slavery.

"Today, we are reporting that this research found that, between 1831 and 1865, two of our predecessor banks — Citizens Bank and Canal Bank in Louisiana — accepted approximately 13,000 enslaved individuals as collateral on loans and took ownership of approximately 1,250 of them when the plantation owners defaulted on the loans," the company wrote in a statement. *(Ref; Atlanta Black Star)*

(Free Slave labor cont);

J.P Morgan & Co.

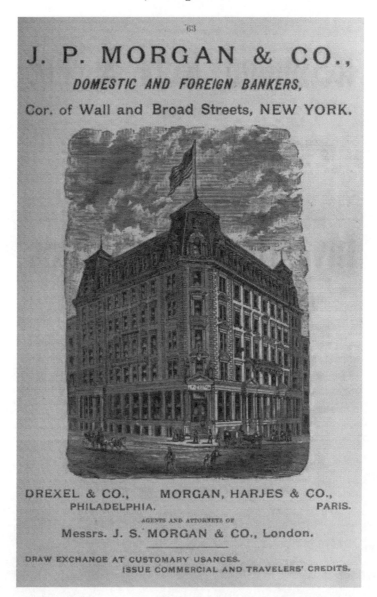

J.P Morgan & Co estimated valued worth 2020 $315.49billion

(Free Slave labor cont);

New York Life Insurance

New York Life Insurance Corp is the third largest life insurance company in the United States , the largest mutual life insurance company in the United States, with assets with a upward 593billion total.

New York Life Insurance Company is the largest mutual life insurance company in the United States. They also took part in slavery by selling insurance policies on enslaved Africans.According to USA Today, evidence of 10 more New York Life slave policies comes from an 1847 account book kept by the company's Natchez, Miss., agent, W.A. Britton. The book, part of a collection at Louisiana State University, contains Britton's notes on slave policies he wrote for amounts ranging from $375 to $600. A 1906 history of New York Life says 339 of the company's first 1,000 policies were written on the lives of slaves.

(Ref, Atlanta Black Star)

(Free Slave labor cont);

Wachovia Bank

WACHOVIA LOAN AND TRUST COMPANY BUILDING.

Wachovia Corporation began on June 16, 1879 in <u>Winston-Salem, North Carolina</u> as the Wachovia National Bank. The bank was co-founded by James Alexander Gray and William Lemly.[10] In 1911, the bank merged with Wachovia Loan and <u>Trust Company</u>, "the largest trust company between <u>Baltimore</u> and <u>New Orleans</u>",[11] which had been founded on June 15, 1893. Wachovia grew to become one of the largest banks in the Southeast partly on the strength of its accounts from the <u>R.J. Reynolds Tobacco Company</u>, which was also headquartered in Winston-Salem.

USA Today reported that Wachovia Corporation (now owned by Wells Fargo) has apologized for its ties to slavery after disclosing that two of its historical predecessors owned enslaved Africans and accepted them as payment.

(Free Slave labor cont.);

Wachovia Bank cont:

"On behalf of Wachovia Corporation, I apologize to all Americans, and especially to African-Americans and people of African descent," said Ken Thompson, Wachovia chairman and chief executive officer, in the statement. "We are deeply saddened by these findings."

Wachovia to be Acquired by Wells Fargo for $15.1 Billion?

Founded in Winston-Salem, N.C. as Wachovia National Bank on June 16, 1879, Wachovia grew to be one of the largest diversified financial services companies in the United States. It traded on the New York Stock Exchange under the symbol WB.

Wachovia provided a broad range of retail banking and brokerage, asset and wealth management, and corporate and investment banking products and services to customers through 3,300 retail financial centers in 21 states, along with nationwide retail brokerage, mortgage lending, and auto finance businesses. Globally, Wachovia served clients in corporate and institutional sectors and through more than 40 international offices.

Wachovia is acquired

In 2008, Wells Fargo & Company acquired Wachovia Corporation to create North America's most extensive distribution system for financial services, Wells Fargo provides banking, insurance, investments, mortgage, and consumer and commercial finance through approximately 5,400 branches, more than 13,000 ATMs, the internet (wellsfargo.com), and other distribution channels across North America and internationally. The integration of Wachovia and Wells Fargo is complete, and all Wachovia accounts have been moved to Wells Fargo.

Fleet Boston Financial

Fleet was founded in <u>Providence, Rhode Island</u> in 1791 as the **Providence Bank** by Rhode Island businessman <u>John Brown</u>. It joined the national banking system in 1865 as Providence National Bank. In 1951, it bought Union Trust Company to form Providence Union Bank and Trust Company. Three years later, it bought Industrial Trust Company to form Industrial National Bank. In 1968, it became the leading subsidiary of Industrial National Corporation.

According to reports, **FleetBoston** evolved from an earlier financial institution, Providence Bank, founded by a John Brown, who was a slave trader and owned ships used to transport enslaved Africans.

The bank financed Brown's slave voyages and profited from them. Brown even reportedly helped charter what became Brown University.

(Free Slave labor cont);

CSX Railways Transportation

The CSX family tree began on **February 28, 1827**, when the Baltimore & Ohio Railroad, America's first common carrier railroad, was chartered. Its original line covered one state and 13 miles; today CSX covers 23 states on our 21,000-mile network. 1827 Baltimore & Ohio began operations on May 24, 1830, as the first common-carrier railroad in the U.S.

CSX used slave labor to construct portions of some U.S. rail lines under the political and legal system that was in place more than a century ago.

Two enslaved Africans whom the company rented were identified as John Henry and Reuben. The record states, "they were to be returned clothed when they arrived to work for the company."

Individual enslaved Africans cost up to $200 — the equivalent of $3,800 today — to rent for a season and CSX took full advantage. *(Ref; Atlanta Black Star)*

(Free Slave labor cont);

Brown Brothers Harriman

Brown Brothers Harriman & Co. (BBH) is the oldest and one of the largest private banks in the United States. In 1931, the merger of Brown Brothers & Co. (founded in 1818) and Harriman Brothers & Co. formed the current BBH. Brown Brothers Harriman is also notable for the number of influential American politicians, government appointees, and Cabinet members who have worked at the company, such as W. Averell Harriman, Prescott Bush, Robert A. Lovett, Richard W. Fisher, Robert Roosa, and Alan Greenspan.

Brown Brothers Harriman is the oldest and largest private investment bank and securities firm in the United States, founded in 1818. USA Today found that the New York merchant bank of James and William Brown, currently known as Brown Bros. Harriman owned hundreds of enslaved Africans and financed the cotton economy by lending millions to southern planters, merchants and cotton brokers. *Assets as of Sept 2016 4.2 trillion.* *(Ref, Atlanta Black Star)*

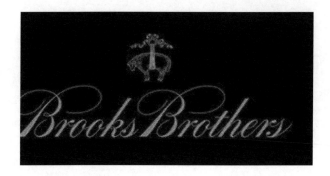

Brooks Brothers

Brooks Brothers is the oldest men's clothier in the United States and is headquartered on Madison Avenue in Manhattan, New York City. Founded in 1818 as a family business, the privately owned company is owned by the Italian billionaire Claudio Del Vecchio. The brand also produces clothing for women, and Zac Posen has been its creative director since June 2014. The company filed for Chapter 11 bankruptcy protection in July 2020, squeezed by the global COVID-19 pandemic and shift towards casual office attire.

Brooks Brothers, the high-end suit retailer, got their start selling slave clothing to various slave traders back in the 1800s. What a way to get rich in the immoral slave industry! *(Ref: Atlanta Black Star)*

(Free Slave labor cont);

Tiffany & Co.

Tiffany &Co. History

"The Diamond King," Charles Lewis Tiffany, introduced the
engagement ring in 1848 in New York City.

Tiffany and Company became known for its diamonds worldwide.

Not only has diamonds for both women and men
- -Jewelry
- -Watches
- -Fragrances,
- -Household items
- -And other accessories.

Reaches a very diverse audience using different social
network sites and tools to increase their consumer reach
and promote new products.

Tiffany and Co. was originally financed with profits from a Connecticut cotton mill. The mill operated from cotton picked by slaves. *(Ref, Race, Racism, and The Law)*

Slavery after slavery

The Devils Punch Bowl, Natchez Mississippi

After slavery was abolished by the 13th Amendment, southern plantation owners were desperate for field labor. A system was devised that resurrected slavery by other means. Slavery had been abolished in every case except "as punishment for crime." White landowners used the South's criminal courts to compel African Americans to work. The South enacted interlocking laws that defined all blacks as criminals, regardless of their behavior, making it legal to press them into chain gangs, labor camps, and other forms of involuntary servitude.

Natchez Mississippi 1865, over 20,000 free Blacks were forced back into slave concentration camps and left for dead in less than a year. "the devils punchbowl"

Vagrancy was defined loosely, so any freed slave not under the protection of a white man could be arrested. An 1865 Mississippi law required black workers to enter into labor contracts with white farmers by January 1 of each year or face arrest. Laws were passed that made it illegal for a black servant to take a job without a discharge paper from his former employer. It was a crime for a black man to speak loudly, have a gun in his pocket, be a bastard or gamble. A crime to walk beside a railroad line, fail to yield a sidewalk to whites, sell cotton after sunset or sell his crop to anyone except his landlord. A crime to sit among whites, and—the greatest sin—to show affection for a white woman.

All were grounds for arrest.

Tens of thousands of black men and boys were forced into labor camps, and criminals were sold into slavery. When complaints were filed it was discovered, slavery might be unconstitutional, but there were no federal statutes making it illegal. White farmers could "lease" as many black workers as they needed. Huge numbers were kidnapped. As these laws expanded, they became the primary means of terrorizing black Americans.

Black tenant farmers never saw wages because charges for rent and food (at company stores like the one run by my friend's father) always exceeded compensation.

Hundreds of thousands of blacks worked in virtual slavery until World War II, and things haven't been exactly sunny for poor African Americans since.

Young child tied to a wooden post and tortured, Natchez Mississippi 1865, Black concentration Camps

The Devils Punch Bowl, Natchez, Mississippi 1865

Black Slaves captured after the civil war and forced into labor camps

The Devil's Punchbowl is a place located in Natchez, Mississippi where during the Civil War; authorities forced tens of thousands of freed slaves to live into concentration camps. Westbrook adds that, "The union army did not allow them to remove the bodies from the camp. They just gave 'em shovels and said bury 'em where they drop."

According to researcher Paula Westbrook, she researched through Adams County Sheriff's reports from the time. "When the slaves were released from the plantations during the occupation they overran Natchez. And the population went from about 10,000 to 120,000 overnight," Westbrook said.

"So they decided to build an encampment for 'em at Devil's Punchbowl which they walled off and wouldn't let 'em out," Don Estes, former director of the Natchez City Cemetery, said.

Estes said that history research is his life. During his studies he said he learned that Union troops ordered re-captured black men to perform hard labor. Women and children were all but left to die in the three "punchbowls"."Disease broke out among 'em, smallpox being the main one. And thousands and thousands died. They were begging to get out. 'Turn me loose and I'll go home back to the plantation! Anywhere but there'," Estes said.

You think concentration camps started with the Nazis? Read on...

In the 1860's, untold numbers of freed slaves were reportedly forced into American concentration camps as they made their way to freedom. They were rounded up, and some lynched, others killed, or many forced back into hard labor and subjected to torture. These contraband camps were hastily built next to Union army camps. Yes, *Union* army! The same group of men who claimed to be fighting to free slaves in the name of humanity.
Did you know the Union army subjected the freed slaves to even worse than slavery? As if that could be fathomed.

Our official educators and the mainstream media have intentionally buried this story, and very little detailed information is readily available on searching. This is not surprising as it casts the Union army in a new light, plus makes one re-evaluate the real motive for the Civil War instead of the fairy tale fed to our children in school.

These camps were in Natchez, Mississippi located in an area known as the Devil's Punchbowl. Here, over 20,000 freed slaves died in this Union army concentration camp. These men, women, and children not even given a proper burial. Shovels were left for the living to bury the bodies where they dropped. Can you imagine bodies buried in the camp where men, women, and children lived?

Black people, overjoyed at being free at last, only to be forced into conditions worse than they had left. It was something none of them could have conceived. Thousands begged to return to slavery. No wonder some call this 'The Black Holocaust'!

(Ref: The Devils Punch Bowl The Hidden History of The Union Army; Failure to Listen a Cultural Blog)

The Devils Punch Bowl 1865

Thousands of Blacks were re-captured and brought back into a worse slavery called "Black Concentration Camps, known as The Devils Punch Bowl located in Natchez Mississippi, were literally thousands of men, women and children were "worked to death", left and for dead.

Today known as just a "Scientific Study Area" still remains the land area of The Devils Punch Bowl, located in Natchez Mississippi

Devils Punch Bowl

Today Natchez Mississippi

Today the area of the landmark site of The Devils Punch Bowl burial grounds

American Presidents that owned and traded Black slaves

This is a **list of presidents of the United States who owned slaves**. Slavery was legal in the United States from its beginning as a nation, having been practiced in North America from early colonial days. The Thirteenth Amendment to the United States Constitution formally abolished slavery in 1865, immediately after the end of the American Civil War.

In total, twelve U.S. presidents owned slaves at some point in their lives; of these, eight owned slaves while in office. George Washington was the first president who owned slaves, including while he was president. Zachary Taylor was the last who owned slaves during his presidency, and Ulysses S. Grant was the last president to have owned a slave at some point in his life. Of those presidents who were slave holders, Thomas Jefferson owned the most, with 600+ slaves, followed by George Washington, with 317 slaves.

Published by Aaron O'Neill, Jul 29, 2020

 Of the first eighteen presidents of the United States, twelve owned slaves throughout their lifetime, and eight of these were slave owners while occupying the office of president. Of the U.S.' first twelve presidents, the only two never to own slaves were John Adams, and his son John Quincy Adams; the first of which famously said that the American Revolution would not be complete until all slaves were freed. George Washington, leader of the revolution and the first President of the United States, owned many slaves throughout his lifetime, with 123* at the time of his death. Historians believe that Washington's treatment of his slaves was typical of slaveowners in Virginia at the time, however he did develop moral issues with the institution of slavery following the revolution. Washington never publicly expressed his growing opposition to slavery, although he did stipulate in his will that all his slaves were to be freed following the death of his wife, and he made financial provisions for their care that lasted until the 1830s.

Jefferson controversies

In recent years, the legacy of Thomas Jefferson has come under the most scrutiny in relation to this matter; the man who penned the words "all men are created equal" is estimated to have owned at least 600 slaves throughout the course of his lifetime. Before becoming president, Jefferson argued for restrictions on the slave trade, and against its expansion into new US territories; however he avoided the subject during his presidency as the topic grew in divisiveness and he believed that emancipation would not be achieved during his lifetime. It is also widely accepted that Jefferson had an affair and likely fathered children with one of his slaves, Sally Hemmings, who is also believed to be the half-sister of Jefferson's first wife. DNA tests conducted in the 1990s confirmed a genetic link between the descendants of the Jefferson and Hemings families, but could not confirm whether the link was Jefferson himself or a relative; most historians however, believe that Jefferson fathered at least one of Sally Hemings' children, and possibly six or eight of them (all of whom were kept as Jefferson's slaves).

Other Presidents

Of the other presidents who appear on this list, all are regarded differently for their attitudes towards slavery, and their impact on the eventual abolition of slavery and the emancipation of slaves. Madison and Monroe grew up in slave-owning families, and owned a number of slaves while serving in the White House; interestingly, Monrovia, the capital city of Liberia (the country was founded by the American Colonization Society as an African settlement for freed slaves), was named in Monroe's honor as he was a prominent advocate of the ACS. Andrew Jackson, who earned a large portion of his private wealth via the slave trade, introduced legislation that protected slave owners and slavery in the southern states; he owned around 200 slaves at the time of his death, and many more throughout his lifetime. John Tyler publicly decried slavery and claimed that it was evil, although he owned slaves as he said this and his political actions in his later life actually supported the institution of slavery (Tyler is notably the only U.S. president whose death was not mourned officially as he was involved in the government of the Confederacy at the time).

Perhaps the most surprising names on this list are Andrew Johnson and Ulysses S Grant, the vice president and leader of the United States Army during the latter stages of the American Civil War. Neither men owned slaves while in office, although Johnson, the man who oversaw the ratification of the Thirteenth Amendment, is reported to have owned eight slaves before entering the world of politics. Ulysses S. Grant, who managed his wife's family's farm in the 1850s, inherited one slave in 1854 who he then freed two years later. Grant's armies would eventually free countless slaves in the 1860s, as he led the Union to victory against the Confederacy and brought an end to slavery in the United States.

Names and amount of Slaves owned by U.S Presidents

1	George Washington	317	Yes (1789–1797)	Washington was a major slaveholder before, during, and after his presidency. His will freed his slaves pending the death of his widow, though she freed them within a year of her husband's death. See George Washington and slavery for more details.
3	Thomas Jefferson	600+	Yes (1801–1809)	Most historians believe Jefferson fathered multiple slave children with the enslaved woman Sally Hemings, the likely half-sister of his late wife Martha Wayles Skelton. Despite being a lifelong slave owner, Jefferson routinely condemned the institution of slavery, attempted to restrict its expansion, and advocated gradual emancipation. As President, he oversaw the abolition of the international slave trade. See Thomas Jefferson and slavery for more details.
4	James Madison	100+	Yes (1809–1817)	Madison proposed the Three-Fifths Compromise, which counted three out of every five slaves for the purposes of taxation and legislative representation. He

				did not free his slaves in his will. Paul Jennings, one of Madison's slaves, served him during his presidency and later published the first memoir of life in the White House.
5	James Monroe	75	Yes (1817–1825)	Monroe supported sending freed slaves to the new country of Liberia; its capital, Monrovia, is named after him. See James Monroe#Slavery for more details.
7	Andrew Jackson	200	Yes (1829–1837)	Jackson owned many slaves. One controversy during his presidency was his reaction to anti-slavery tracts. During his campaign for the presidency, he faced criticism for being a slave trader. He did not free his slaves in his will.
8	Martin Van Buren	1	No (1837–1841)	Van Buren's father owned six slaves. The only slave he personally owned, Tom, escaped in 1814. When Tom was found in Massachusetts, Van Buren tentatively agreed to sell him to the finder, but terms were not agreed and Tom remained free. Later in life, Van Buren belonged to the Free Soil Party, which opposed the expansion of slavery into the Western territories without advocating immediate abolition.
9	William Henry Harrison	11	No (1841)	Harrison inherited several slaves. As the first governor of the Indiana Territory, he unsuccessfully lobbied Congress to legalize slavery in Indiana.

10	John Tyler	70	Yes (1841–1845)	Tyler never freed any of his slaves and consistently supported slavery and its expansion during his time in political office.
11	James K. Polk	25	Yes (1845–1849)	Polk became the Democratic nominee for president in 1844 partially because of his tolerance of slavery, in contrast to Van Buren. As president, he generally supported the rights of slave owners. His will provided for the freeing of his slaves after the death of his wife, though the Emancipation Proclamation and the Thirteenth Amendment to the United States Constitution ended up freeing them long before her death in 1891.
12	Zachary Taylor	< 150	Yes (1849–50)	Although Taylor owned slaves throughout his life, he generally resisted attempts to expand slavery in the territories. After his death, there were rumors that slavery advocates had poisoned him; tests of his body over 100 years later have been inconclusive.
17	Andrew Johnson	8	No (1865–1869)	Johnson owned a few slaves and was supportive of James K. Polk's slavery policies. As military governor of Tennessee, he convinced Abraham Lincoln to exempt that area from the Emancipation Proclamation.
18	Ulysses S. Grant	1	No (1869–1877)	Although he later served as a general in the Union Army, his wife Julia had control of four slaves during the American Civil War, given to her by her father. However, it is unclear if she actually was granted legal ownership of them or merely temporary

				custody.[2] All would be freed by the Emancipation Proclamation of 1863 (she chose to free them at that time even though the proclamation did not apply to her state of Missouri).[3] Grant personally owned one slave, William Jones, given to him in 1857 by his father-in-law and <u>manumitted</u> by Grant on March 29, 1859.[4]

The Berry Hill Slave Plantation, South Boston, VA

The Berry Hill Slave Plantation, built 1839

SANKOFA'S SLAVERY DATA COLLECTION

Berry Hill Plantation

Location: Woodbourne, Halifax Co., VA
Constructed: 1770

History: In ante-bellum days the Berry Hill plantation comprised over five thousand acres, and included most of present-day South Boston. Its various tracts were acquired partly by James Bruce of Woodbourne, one of the wealthiest men of his day, and partly by James Coles Bruce, his son by his first wife, Sarah 'Sally' Coles, daughter of Walter Coles, Esq., of Mildendo. James built the great family fortune through what was then a very modern medium--a system of chain stores. At the early age of sixteen he left the relative comfort and security of Soldier's Rest and went to Petersburg, where he began his career in the mercantile house of a Mr. Colquhoun. He easily won the confidence of his employer, and was sent to Amelia County to open a branch store, in which he was made a partner. After a few years James found that the more remote areas of Halifax County offered far greater business advantages, so settled there 1798 and began setting up his stores, not only in the county but in the surrounding counties of both Virginia and North Carolina as well, to supply the needs of the rural planters. To furnish his stores with their wares, Mr. Bruce also operated a series of wagon trains.

The late Dr. Kathleen Bruce, family historian and a noted writer, made an exhaustive study of her great-grandfather's papers, and revealed that between the years 1802 and 1837, James was the owner or dominant partner in, among other enterprises, twelve country stores, several flour mills, a fertilizer-plaster manufactory, a commercial blacksmith shop, several lumber yards, a cotton factory and two taverns. When he died in 1837 James Bruce was the third wealthiest man in America, his estate being valued at nearly three million dollars. Death came to James Bruce in Philadelphia, where he had gone for medical treatment, and as it was impractical to transport bodies such great distances in those days, he was buried in the yard of old St. Andrew's Episcopal Church. (Nearly one hundred years later his great-grandson, Malcolm Bruce, had his remains brought back to Halifax County and interred at Berry Hill.) The widowed Elvira Cabell Henry Bruce (James Bruce of Woodbourne's second wife) soon left Woodbourne and moved her family to Richmond, where she built a house on fashionable East Clay Street.

(Berry Hill Plantation cont);

The Berry Hill Slave Plantation the ruins of slave quarters still remain today

Diamond Hill Cemetery the oldest Black slave cemetery in America, located on the Berry Hill plantation, South Boston, VA

Chapter three

The Unmentioned History of Terrorism on Blacks in America

Blacks in America have been faced with centuries of unfair, and unmentionable torture, heinous intentional murders, and the shedding of innocent blood at the hands of White Americans. These centuries of mandated well throughout senseless murders have not only been overlooked but these are acts of blatant terrorism at its worse. Blacks, Natives, and Latinos have not only suffered the worse treatment more so than any group of people throughout this earth, but these acts of terrorism have not only been over-looked, but the American society has placed these acts of murder as "acts of cruelty', or possibly " racially motivated acts of hate", or "Hate Crimes" as of late. But on the contrary Blacks Americans have suffered more acts of terrorism than any group or nation of people that has existed until this very day.

These historical facts, articles, along with voices of eye witnesses are some of the most shocking acts of terrorism leveled on Blacks that society, and the educational systems of America has intentionally hid from the eyes and readers of Black Americans. This is what they will not teach you in school. Below are actual written reported articles of some accounts of lynches of Blacks, just imagine how many were unreported?

Thousands of Blacks lynched

"Neither slavery nor involuntary servitude, except as a punishment for crime whereof the party shall have been duly convicted, shall exist within the United States, or any place subject to their jurisdiction," the amendment says.
For blacks, the moment represented liberty in its truest form — the country's defining document now outlawed slavery. But the 13th Amendment infuriated many Southern whites who refused to accept the outcome of the Civil War.
The next 12 years during the period known as Reconstruction was one of the most brutal stretches of organized racial terrorism in American history, with white mobs attacking and lynching blacks. The unprovoked assaults stretched into the early 1950s. (*Ref The Washington Post, by Michael S. Rosenwald*)

Historians have struggled for years to figure out just how many blacks were lynched. Now, thanks to a new report from the Equal Justice Initiative, the numbers are coming into clearer focus. The Alabama-based organization <u>said its researchers have documented</u> 6,500 lynchings between 1865 and 1950, including 2,000 attacks during Reconstruction that weren't tallied in its <u>previous reports</u>.

Thousands of other blacks were also assaulted and raped, the organization said. And the actual number of attacks might never be known.
"Emboldened Confederate veterans and former enslavers organized a reign of terror that effectively nullified constitutional amendments designed to provide Black people with equal protection and the right to vote," the report said.
"Violence, mass lynchings, and lawlessness enabled white Southerners to create a regime of white supremacy and Black disenfranchisement alongside a new economic order that continued to exploit Black labor." *(Ref: Washington Post, by Michael S. Rosenwald)*

1937

Duck Hill, Mississippi, "Boot Jack McDaniel's" lynched in front of 500 white men, women, and children.

(Terrorism on Blacks cont);

Two Negroes Are Lynched By 500 Whites (1937)

Pair Killed in Mississippi After Pleading Innocent to Murder Charge

Winona, Miss., April 13 – While women, and even little children, looked upon the gruesome scene, two negroes accused of murdering a white merchant, were tortured with fire and lynched by a frenzied mob of nearly 500 persons near Duck Hill, this afternoon.

A third negro suspected by the mob in the slaying of George Windham, a county storekeeper, was severely whipped and run out of the county after narrowly escaping the mob's vicious vengeance. A negro, identified only as "Bootjack" McDaniels, indicted with Townes in the Windham slaying, was shot by members of the mob, and his body burned.

Townes and McDaniels were taken from Sheriff E. E. Wright and two deputies early this afternoon as they were being led from the courtroom to be returned to the jail to await trial Thursday. "It was all done quickly, quietly and orderly," said Deputy Sheriff A.J. Curtis, one of the officers overpowered by the mob. Curtis said that when the prisoners were led out of the courthouse door, a group of men milling about the courtyard closed in on the sheriff, his two deputies and the prisoners.

"Two men grabbed my arms and pinned them behind me," he said. "The other officers were overpowered in the same way. There was no other form of violence, and no effort was made at shooting," the officer said.

Curtis said the men were not masked, but said he did not recognize any of the men.

The negroes were handcuffed, and placed in a waiting school bus. Members of the mob piled into the bus, and others into automobiles. The caravan sped northward toward Duck Hill and to the site of George Windham's small store, where the white man was fatally shot through a window last December.

As the caravan proceeded along the highway, the line of cars lengthened. One Winona citizen who would not permit the use of his name said "there must have been 500 men there before it was all over."

(Terrorism on Blacks cont);

1937 Duck Hill, Mississippi the lynching of Boot Jack McDaniel's and Roosevelt Towns

The caravan sped northward toward Duck Hill as the negroes screamed for mercy. The bus stopped near the small country store where Windham was fatally shot through a window one night last December. Then the negroes were tied to a tree and tortured.Townes' eyes were gouged out with an ice pick and a blow torch was applied to parts of his body before he died.McDaniels was flogged by members of the mob who took turns with chain and a horsewhip. Still alive, he was riddled with buckshot. Everett Dorroh, Negro farmer, happened to be passing the scene and was attracted by the crowd. Before he had fathomed what was going on or had a chance to leave, he was named by someone in the mob as an accomplice in the white man's murder. Dorroh was flogged and told to run. Buckshot was fired at him and some entered his leg but he somehow managed to escape with his life.

(Terrorism on black's cont.);

Wiona Miss, Press 1937

Blacks Blow Torched Duck Hill, Mississippi

The Laura Nelson Lynching, Okfuskee County, Oklahoma May 25th 1911

Laura and L.D. Nelson (born 1878 and 1897)[2] were an African-American mother and son who were lynched on May 25, 1911, near Okemah, the county seat of Okfuskee County, Oklahoma.[3]

Laura, her husband Austin, their teenage son L.D., and possibly their child had been taken into custody after George Loney, Okemah's deputy sheriff, and three others arrived at the Nelsons' home on May 2, 1911, to investigate the theft of a cow. The son shot Loney, who was hit in the leg and bled to death; Laura was reportedly the first to grab the gun and was charged with murder, along with her son. Her husband pleaded guilty to larceny, and was sent to the relative safety of the state prison in McAlester. The son L.D. Nelson was held in the county jail in Okemah and the mother Laura in a cell in the nearby courthouse to await trial.[4]

At around midnight on May 24, Laura and L.D. Nelson were both kidnapped from their cells by a group of between a dozen and 40 men; the group included Charley Guthrie (1879–1956), the father of folk singer Woody Guthrie (1912–1967), according to a statement given in 1977 by the former's brother.[5] *The Crisis*, the magazine of the National Association for the Advancement of Colored People, said in July 1911 that Laura was raped, then she and L.D. were hanged from a bridge over the North Canadian River.[6] According to some sources, Laura had a baby with her at the time, who one witness said survived the attack.[7]

Sightseers gathered on the bridge the following morning and photographs of the hanging bodies were sold as postcards; the one of Laura is the only known surviving photograph of a female lynching victim.[8] No one was ever charged with the murders; the district judge convened a grand jury, but the killers were never identified.[9] Although Woody Guthrie was not born until 14 months after the lynching, the photographs and his father's reported involvement had a lasting effect on him, and he wrote several songs about the killings.[(

The Jim Redmond, Gus Roberson, Bob Addison Lynching

1892

ATLANTA, Ga, May 18.—Details of the lynching at Clarksville of Jim Redmond, Gus Robinson and Bob Anderson, colored, for the murder of Marshal Carter has been received. They were taken from the jail by a mob estimated at from 100 to 500, who overpowered the Sheriff and his guards. Redmond and Addison [sic] begged piteously for mercy, but Robinson never opened his mouth. The negroes were carried about a mile and a half from the jail and the mob stopped. Three long trace chains and three padlocks were produced, and the chains were locked around the negroes' necks. Then Redmond was made to stand upon a horse under a limb of a tree. A man who had climbed the tree made the chain fast and Redmond was questioned about the killing. He repeated the same story he first told.

"Let the horse go," said the leader of the mob. Someone touched the horse with a whip and he sprang from under Redmond. As the negro went down he exclaimed: "Lord have mercy on my soul." Addison came next, but he denied all knowledge of the crime. Just before the horse moved, he dropped off and fell the full length of the chain. Robinson was put upon the horse and asked the same questions which had been propounded to the others. "All I know I'll die and go to — knowing," he said, "before I'll tell." The horse was touched and Robinson went down. His neck was broken, while the other two died of strangulation. The bodies were left hanging side by side until 3 o'clock this afternoon. The verdict was death from unknown hands

(*Ref. Strange Fruit and Spanish Moss, Reported by The daily Review, Decatur, Illinois dated May 19th, 1892*)

1892, May 17th, Atlanta Georgia, *(Ref: Strange Fruit and Spanish Moss, Reported by The Daily Review (Decatur, Illinois dated May 19th 1892)*

(Terrorism on Blacks cont):

1902

The lynching of Garfield Burley and Curtis Brown, 1902 October 8th Tennessee

1906

This photograph shows five African American men who have been lynched, North Carolina, 6 August 1906. Nease and John Gillespie, Jack Dillingham, Henry Lee and George Irwin are the victims of a brutal era where African Americans were frequently unprotected by the law, murdered by White Americans and denied justice by the American criminal justice system. There were a reported over 6000-7000 reported lynchings of Blacks between that late 1700's-late 1800's, Negroes were slaves here in America two centuries prior to the reported count, just imagine the un-reported amount?

1919

In Omaha, Nebraska on 28 September 1919 a mob of over five thousand Americans surrounded and attacked a county court house and seized an innocent African American accused of assaulting a 'white' girl. The mob mutilated him, shooting him over a thousand times before burning his body. Subsequently there were twenty five major race riots across the US in the last six months of 1919. The taking of 'trophy' photos was popular at this time.

1920 Lige Daniels

1920 August 3rd, Texas, 16 year old Black youth Lige Daniels hung in public

(Terrorism on Blacks cont.);

Ruben Stacy

(Ref, The Ruben Stacy Story; A media on Lynching, Black Youth)

Ruben Stacy 1935 July 19th Florida

Rubin Stacy, a man born between 1899-1907 in Georgia. He left Georgia to go to Florida where there were more opportunities. Unfortunately, he was murdered July 19, 1935 in Fort Lauderdale. He was murdered because he was falsely accused of trying to harm Marion Jones, a white woman. She later reported that he came to her door begging for food. In the foreground of the photo, you see—the bloodied body of—our Rubin hanging from a tree. In the background, you see a group of whites milling about looking on with glee at the *STRANGE FRUIT*. In the group of children, you can see this little white girl smiling angelically up at the beaten, swollen and patently dead face of Rubin Stacy. In addition to the pain endured by Rubin, I want to focus on this white girl, her angelic smile, her Sunday's best wears, and her clan of 'law-abiding' white folks. This iconic image captures what we collaboratively seek to forget in order to embrace this color-blind, post-racial and multi-culti society.

Yeah, that's right, 'the white family next door' was responsible for Rubin's hanging not the Klan. What's more horrifying to note is that in these lynching rituals the town's people protected each other and often in the police and coroner's records these crimes are often cited as killed "at the hands of persons unknown." So how would you explain the little white girl's smile when we can presume that she is not a child of a Klan member?(*Ref. The Ruben Stacy Story: A Media on Lynching Post Racial America, Black youth*)

Ruben Stacey murdered 1935, Florida

PHILADELPHIA INQUIRER
January 3, 1916

BLACKS LYNCHED FOR REMARK
WHICH MAY HAVE BEEN "HELLO"

HARTWELL, Ga., Jan. 2—Two negroes were lynched and a negro woman was badly beaten as the result of a remark to a white girl in Anderson County, South Carolina, according to reports received here tonight.

The three negroes were riding in a buggy when they passed the girl. One of the men made a remark to the white girl, at which she took offense. She reported the encounter to a group of white men who quickly caught up with the blacks, lynched the men, beat the woman and ordered her out of the state.

Reports concerning the nature of the allegedly insulting remark are conflicting. Officials of Georgia county say that one of the negro men yelled out, "Hello, Sweetheart." The negro woman asserts that all they said was "Hello."

ATLANTA CONSTITUTION
January 3, 1916

NEGRO CHURCH AND LODGES
BURNED AFTER 6 LYNCHINGS

BLAKELY, Ga., Jan. 2—While no more attempts have been made on the lives of negroes since last week's outbreak, in which six negroes were killed, reports reached here today that a negro church building, in the western part of this (Early) county, was burned last night. Some half dozen lodge buildings have been burned since angry whites went out to avenge the death of Henry J. Villipigue, an overseer residing in the western part of the county, but until last night, negro churches, it was said, had been spared. Villipigue was murdered by negroes for having whipped one of them, according to statements by neighbors.

98

(Ref: Philadelphia Inquirer Jan 3, 1916, Atlanta Constitution Jan 3, 1916),100 Years of lynchings, by Ralph Ginzburg, page 98.

NEW YORK HERALD

January 22, 1916

FIVE LYNCHED IN GEORGIA

SYLVESTER, Ga., Friday—The bullet-riddled bodies of five negroes found hanging from a tree near Starkville, Ga., to-day, increased the total of negroes lynched in that section to fourteen within the last five weeks. The victims of the latest lynching were accused by a mob of having knowledge of the killing of Sheriff Moreland of Lee County.

Four of the victims were of one family—Felix Lake and his three sons, Frank, Dewer and Major. The fifth victim was Rodius Seamore.

ATLANTA CONSTITUTION

February 23, 1916

ALL FIVE LYNCHED NEGROES WERE GUILTLESS, SAYS KEITH

TIFTON, Ga., Feb. 22—Jim Keith, sentenced to a life term in prison for complicity in the killing of Sheriff Moreland of Lee county, talked freely of the crime today as he was carried to Richmond county to begin serving his term. He declared that Rodius Seamore and old man

99

(Ref, New York Herald Jan 22, 1916, Atlanta Constitution February 23, 1916)

(100 Hundred Years of lynchings, by Ralph Ginzburg page 99)

SEATTLE TIMES
March 31, 1914

COLORED WOMAN IS HANGED

MUSKOGEE, Okla., Mar. 31—Marie Scott, a negro woman, was taken from the Wagoner County jail early today and hanged to a telephone pole.

A mob of at least a dozen armed men overpowered the jailer, a one-armed man, threw a rope over the screaming woman's head, dragged her out of her cell and strung her up a block from the jail.

Marie Scott was charged with driving a knife into the heart of Lemuel Peace, a youthful white man who, in company with other young white men, had gone to the negro quarter of Wagoner last Saturday night.

BOSTON GUARDIAN
April 30, 1914

NEGRO YOUTH MUTILATED FOR KISSING WHITE GIRL

MARSHALL, Tex., Apr. 29—Because he is alleged to have hugged and kissed a white girl, daughter of a farmer, Charles Fisher, a negro youth, was recently badly mutilated by a mob near here. According to Sheriff Sanders and County Health Officer Taylor, the mob sheared off the youth's ears, slit his lips and mutilated him in other ways below the belt.

(Reported by Seattle Times March 31, 1914, Muskogee, OK, Reported by Boston Guardian April 30 1914, Marshall, TX), 100Years Of Lynchings by Ralph Ginzburg

MONTGOMERY ADVERTISER
May 8, 1914

SHOE THIEF SUSPECT LYNCHED

GROVETON, Ga., May 7—Charley Jones, a negro, was taken from two officers near here late last night by a number of white men and lynched. It is said that Jones was suspected of having shop lifted a pair of shoes.

ATLANTA CONSTITUTION
July 1, 1914

TWO ACCIDENTALLY KILLED IN SWAMP HUNT FOR NEGRO

SHAW, Miss., June 30—A member of the posse hunting for Jack Farmer, negro, was accidentally shot and killed by a fellow member of the posse early today. Fred Young mistook James Jolly, a fellow posseman, for Farmer as they were both pushing their way through a swamp here where it was believed Farmer was hiding.

91

(Ref Montgomery Advertiser May 8 1914, Grovetin, GA, Ref Atlanta Constitution July 1 1914, Shaw, Miss)

CLEVELAND GAZETTE
December 13, 1914

LA. NEGRO IS BURNED ALIVE SCREAMING "I DIDN'T DO IT"

SHREVEPORT, La., Dec. 12—Charred remains of Watkins Lewis, the third negro to die at the hands of mobs as the result of the murder of Charles Hicks, postmaster at Sylvester, La., last week, were found today near Sylvester bound to a tree with coils of wire. The burning of Lewis makes a total of eight lynchings in this parish in the last year, five negroes having been put to death in the last ten days. Tobe Lewis and Monroe Lewis were lynched last week for their alleged part in the Hicks murder.

Stories here tonight tell of a mob of 200 white men, formed in the outskirts of Sylvester last night. Lewis, cringing with fear, was taken from the jail here, placed in a motor car, and whirled to the mob. Not a word was spoken as the little cavalcade formed, and with the negro in the center marched to a giant tree near the Texas line. Lewis was bound to the trunk. Fallen trees and branches were heaped about him. Before the fire was lighted Lewis repeatedly was asked to confess his part in the crime, or to divulge the hiding place of a large sum of money said to have been stolen from the postmaster's store.

"I didn't do it," he screamed as the flames leaped about him.

When the fire enveloped him the mob dispersed. Today the town of Sylvester was quiet.

93

(*Ref Cleveland Gazette, December 13, 1914, Shreveport, LA), 100 Years of lynchings by ralph Ginzburg*)

CHICAGO TRIBUNE
December 31, 1914

1914 LYNCHINGS SHOW RISE

The number of lynchings in 1914 shows a small increase over that of 1913, being 54, as compared with 48 in 1913 and 64 in 1912. The following table showing the annual number during the last thirty years may be of general interest:

1865	184	1900	115
1886	138	1901	130
1887	122	1902	96
1888	142	1903	104
1889	176	1904	87
1890	127	1905	60
1891	193	1906	60
1892	205	1907	65
1893	200	1908	100
1894	170	1909	87
1895	171	1910	74
1896	181	1911	71
1897	106	1912	64
1898	127	1913	48
1899	107	1914	54

NEW YORK WORLD
February 18, 1915

ANOTHER FLORIDA LYNCHING

TAMPA, Fla., Feb. 17—John Richards, a negro, was lynched by a mob near Sparr, Fla., last night. He is said to have insulted a white woman.

Chicago Tribune reported 1914 lynchings rise; New York World February 18, 1915, Tampa, FL

CHICAGO DEFENDER
February 31, 1915

NEGRO SHOT DEAD FOR KISSING HIS WHITE GIRLFRIEND

CEDAR KEYS, Fla., Feb. 26—Young Reed, Negro, of Kissimee, was shot to death by a white mob at Wednesday noon after he had been seen kissing a white woman named Belle Mann with whom he had been keeping company for the past two years.

Reed was kissing Miss Mann good-bye when he was seen by a group of white men. The men seized him, beat him unmercifully and placed him in jail. Shortly thereafter a lynching party was formed and Reed was shot to death.

Local men of the Negro race have sworn to burn down the homes of white men living with colored women to avenge the death of Reed.

ATLANTA CONSTITUTION
April 18, 1915

CHARGED WITH STEALING MEAT

VALDOSTA, Ga., April 17—Caesar Sheffield, a negro prisoner in the town jail at Lake Park, was taken from the prison last night and shot to death by unknown parties. No trail has been found of the slayers.

Sheffield was arrested yesterday charged with stealing meat from the smokehouse of Elder B. Herring and put in jail to await trial. The prison was forced open by unknown parties and cries were heard from the negro about 9 o'clock last night. Moses Oppenheim, who went to investigate the cries, was driven back by shots fired in his direction, and was unable to identify the men who were making off with the prisoner. Sheffield's body was found this morning in a field near the railroad station at Lake Park.

95

Ref Chicago Defender February 31 1915, Cedar keys, FL, Ref Atlanta Constitution April 18, 1915, Valdosta, GA, '100 Years of lynchings" by Ralph Ginzburg

BIRMINGHAM VOICE OF THE PEOPLE
April 1, 1916

BUMPS INTO GIRL; IS LYNCHED

CEDAR BLUFF, Miss., March 31—Jeff Brown was lynched by a mob here late Saturday afternoon. Brown was walking down the street near the car tracks and saw a moving freight going in the direction in which he wanted to go. He started on the run to board the moving train. On the sidewalk was the daughter of a white farmer. Brown accidentally brushed against her and she screamed. A gang quickly formed and ran after him, jerking him off the moving train. He was beaten into insensibility and then hung to a tree. The sheriff has made no attempt to find out who the members of the mob were. Picture cards of the body are being sold on the streets at five cents apiece.

ATLANTA CONSTITUTION
April 4, 1916

LYNCHED FROM COURTHOUSE

IDABEL, Okla., April 3—After listening to the evidence at the preliminary hearing here today of Oscar Martin, a negro charged with having attacked a 13-year-old girl, a mob of five hundred men overpowered court attaches and hanged the negro from a second story balcony of the courthouse.

Evidently at a previously arranged signal the mob sprang up from among the spectators at the conclusion of the evidence and while court officers were held prisoners, dragged the negro to the balcony from which he was thrown after one end of a rope had been placed around his neck and the other made secure to a post.

The mob dispersed within a few minutes. To-night the town is quiet.

(*Ref. Birmingham Voice of The People, April 1 1916, Cedar Bluff, Miss, Ref; Atlanta Constitution, April 4 1916, Idabel, OK), "100 Years Of lynchings", by Ralph Ginzburg, pg102*

of which Roach was a member comprising about 75 men, has quit. The force was engaged in the construction of sand clay roads in the county. The Negroes declared they will not work any more in Person county.

THE RALEIGH INDEPENDENT
July 17, 1920

NEGRO LYNCHED AT ROXBORO WAS WRONG MAN, SAYS BOSS

DURHAM, July 12—Ed. Roach, the Negro who was lynched by a Person County mob last Wednesday morning was innocent of the crime for which he died, according to a signed statement made by Nello Taylor, widely known contractor and employer of the mob victim.

The infuriated mob, in the opinion of the contractor, made a ghastly mistake when they dragged Roach from the Person County jail, hanged him to the church-yard tree and riddled his body with bullets, while the brute who committed the crime was allowed to escape.

"When this Negro was lynched," Mr. Taylor says in his statement, "as innocent a man was murdered as could have been, had you or I been the victim of the mob."

Continuing, the contractor says: "Roach was working for me and was a quiet, hard-working inoffensive humble Negro. On Monday he came to me and stated that he was sick and wanted to go with me to Durham that night to see a doctor. Instead I arranged for him to go Tuesday night to Roxboro. He continued his work all day Tuesday until 5:30 (Bear in mind that the crime for which he was lynched occurred between 2 and 3 o'clock that afternoon), when he asked permission of his foreman to stop and go to Mt. Tersa station to catch the train for Roxboro. Permission was given him and he left for the station walking. At 5:45 he passed the State's bridge crew (white men) and two men who were out searching for the guilty Negro saw him and followed him up the road to the Mount Tersa station, where he sat down and waited for the train. These two men sat down on the railroad near him. When the train came he got on and paid the conductor his fare to Roxboro and got off the

137

News Article

(Roxboro lynching cont);

train there. He was not arrested until he got off the train. I am advised by the chief of police he asked what they had him for and told them he had not done anything, but he was not told until he got in jail what they had him for. He asked to be taken to my office to see my superintendent with whom he had arranged to carry him to the doctor, but permission was refused him."

Mr. Teer says the right Negro was probably one that worked at his camp only a few hours.

"A Negro man about Roach's size came to my camp on Sunday night, was employed on Monday and went to work Tuesday morning. About 8:15 a. m. he drove my team out to the side of the road and had been gone twenty-five minutes when my foreman missed him. My foreman took out one of the mules and went to look for him, saw him going up the road toward's Mt. Tersa Station, the Negro saw him and broke and ran over on the east side of the railroad, going towards Lynchburg. This was about 10:30 a. m. Tuesday morning and in approximately three-quarters of a mile of the scene of the crime. This man was dressed practically the same as Ed. Roach, with cap and overalls was about the same size, but a little darker in color."

In conclusion Mr. Teer says:

"I make this statement in the interest of truth and justice, yet with a full knowledge of the odium I am bringing down upon my own head in doing so, but with the hope that this fearful crime may so shock our people as to make its likes again an impossibility."

Cont: (Ref. The Raleigh Independent, July 17, 1920)

The Wilmington Massacre 1898

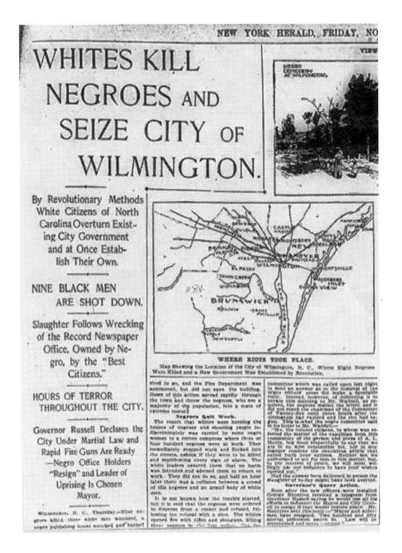

(Ref, The New York Herald reported Nov 11, 1898)

The Wilmington massacre is American Terrorism at its finest. It occurred in North Carolina on Nov. 10 1898

The Wilmington Massacre of 1898 was a bloody attack on the African American community by a heavily armed white mob with the support of the North Carolina Democratic Party on November 10, 1898 in the port city of Wilmington, North Carolina.This event is considered one of the only successful examples of a violent overthrow of an existing government (coup d'etat) and left countless numbers of African American citizens dead and exiled from the city. It was the springboard for the white supremacy movement and Jim Crow Segregation throughout the state of North Carolina, and the American South. This incident is barely mentioned and has been omitted from most history books. It was not until 2006, after the North Carolina General Assembly published a report on it, that the tragedy became known to the public.

(1898) Rev. Charles S. Morris Describes The Wilmington Massacre of 1898.

Nine Negroes massacred outright; a score wounded and hunted like partridges on the mountain; one man, brave enough to fight against such odds would be hailed as a hero anywhere else, was given the privilege of running the gauntlet up a broad street, where he sank ankle deep in the sand, while crowds of men lined the sidewalks and riddled him with a pint of bullets as he ran bleeding past their doors; another Negro shot twenty times in the back as he scrambled empty handed over a fence; thousands of women and children fleeing in terror from their humble homes in the darkness of the night, out under a gray and angry sky, from which falls a cold and bone chilling rain, out to the dark and tangled ooze of the swamp amid the crawling things of night, fearing to light a fire, startled at every footstep, cowering, shivering, shuddering, trembling, praying in gloom and terror: half-clad and barefooted mothers, with their babies wrapped only in a shawl, whimpering with cold and hunger at their icy breasts, crouched in terror from the vengeance of those who, in the name of civilization, and with the benediction of the ministers of the Prince of Peace, inaugurated the reformation of the city of Wilmington the day after the election by driving out one set of white office holders and filling their places with another set of white office holders—the one being Republican and the other Democrat.(*Ref, I love Ancestry Wilmington-massacre-north-Carolina)*

Some of the 2000 white men that led an attack against Blacks in Wilmington, NC killing up to 300 in 1898

The **Wilmington insurrection of 1898**, also known as the **Wilmington massacre of 1898** or the **Wilmington coup of 1898**,[6] occurred in Wilmington, North Carolina, on

Thursday, November 10, 1898.[7] It is considered a turning point in post-Reconstruction North Carolina politics. The event initiated an era of more severe racial segregation and effective disenfranchisement of African Americans throughout the South, a shift already underway since passage by Mississippi of a new constitution in 1890, raising barriers to voter registration. Laura Edwards wrote in *Democracy Betrayed* (2000): "What happened in Wilmington became an affirmation of white supremacy not just in that one city, but in the South and in the nation as a whole", as it affirmed that invoking "whiteness" eclipsed the legal citizenship, individual rights, and equal protection under the law that blacks were guaranteed under the Fourteenth Amendment.[8][9][10]

The white press in Wilmington originally described the event as a race riot caused by blacks. However, over time, with more facts publicized, the event has come to be seen as a *coup d'état*, the violent overthrow of a duly elected government, by a group of white supremacists. Multiple causes brought it about.[1][11][12][13][14][15][16] It is claimed to be the only such incident in American history,[17][18] (other late Reconstruction Era violence did not result in a direct 'coup' or removal and replacement of elected officials by unelected individuals).

The *coup* occurred after the state's white Southern Democrats conspired and led a mob of 2,000 white men to overthrow the legitimately elected local Fusionist government. They expelled opposition black and white political leaders from the city, destroyed the property and businesses of black citizens built up since the Civil War, including the only black newspaper in the city, and killed an estimated 60 to more than 300 people.[2][3][4][5]

In 1860, before the Civil War, Wilmington was majority black and the largest city in the state, with nearly 10,000 people.[19] Numerous enslaved laborers and free people of color worked at the port, in households as domestic servants, and in a variety of jobs as artisans and skilled workers.[19]

In the years that followed,[when?] Wilmington, then the largest city in the state, had a majority-black population, with black people accounting for about 55 percent of its roughly 25,000 people.[24][25] Included were numerous black professionals and businessmen, and a rising middle class.

Blacks also held significant economic power in the city. Many former slaves had skills which they were able to use in the marketplace.[27] For example, several became bakers, grocers, dyers, etc., making up nearly 35 percent of Wilmington's service positions, which was down over 20 percent from 1889.

Black people were moving out of service jobs and into other types of employment, where there was a higher demand for their work, along with higher pay. At the time, black people accounted for over 30 percent of Wilmington's skilled craftsmen, such as mechanics, carpenters, jewelers, watchmakers, painters, plasterers, plumbers, stevedores, blacksmiths, masons, and wheelwrights.[23] In addition, blacks owned ten of the city's 11 restaurants, 90 percent of the city's 22 barbers, and one of the city's four fish and oysters' dealerships. There were also more black bootmakers/shoemakers than white ones, one-third of the city's butchers were black, and half of the city's tailors were black. Lastly, two brothers, Alexander and Frank Manly, owned the *Wilmington Daily Record*, one of the few black newspapers in the state at the time, which was reported to be the only black daily newspaper in the country.

Several homes and businesses of successful blacks would sometimes be torched by whites at night.[23] But because blacks had enough economic and political power to defend their interests, socially, things were relatively peaceful.[23]

The Rosewood Florida Massacre 1923

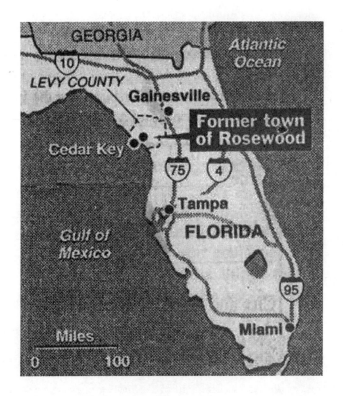

From Wikipedia,

Rosewood is a former populated place in Levy County, Florida, United States. The site is located just off State Road 24, approximately 1 mile (1.6 km) northeast of Sumner and 9 miles (14 km) northeast of Cedar Key. The town was destroyed by whites and subsequently abandoned in 1923

Rosewood was settled in 1845, nine miles (14 km) east of Cedar Key, near the Gulf of Mexico. Local industry centered on timber. The name Rosewood refers to the reddish color of cut cedar wood. Two pencil mills were nearby in Cedar Key; several turpentine mills and a sawmill three miles (4.8 km) away in Sumner helped support local residents, as did farming of citrus and cotton. The hamlet grew enough to warrant the construction of a post office and train depot on the Florida Railroad in 1870, but it was never incorporated as a town.

The population of Rosewood peaked in 1915 at 355 people. Two black families in Rosewood named Goins and Carrier were the most influential. The Goins family brought the turpentine industry to the area, and in the years preceding the attacks, were the second largest landowners in Levy County. To avoid lawsuits from white competitors, the Goins brothers moved to Gainesville, and the population of Rosewood decreased slightly. The Carriers were also a large family, responsible for logging in the region. By the 1920s, almost everyone in the close-knit community was distantly related to each other. Although residents of Rosewood probably did not vote because voter registration requirements in Florida had effectively disfranchised blacks since the turn of the century, both Sumner and Rosewood were part of a single voting precinct counted by the U.S. Census. In 1920, the combined population of both towns was 344 blacks and 294 whites.

The Rosewood Massacre was a series of riots that took place in the small town of Rosewood in Florida, in January 1923. Several black residents of the town were tortured, killed, and wounded during the riots; many houses were burned down, and a number of families were destroyed.

Did You Know?

The official number of blacks killed due to the Rosewood Massacre was 6. However, researchers claim that at least 27 black residents had died, and that the actual number of fatalities was never reported.

The town of Rosewood was settled in 1845, nine miles east to the Cedar Key, Florida, near the Gulf of Mexico. The cultivation of citrus and cotton, as well as the growth of the timber industry, gave rise to the construction of a train depot and a post office in the town, in 1870. Initially, the population of Rosewood included both whites and blacks. However, after the pencil mills in the town were closed, most of the whites migrated to other cities, and by 1900, the population in Rosewood had become predominantly black. By the year 1920, the blacks were in possession of a sugarcane mill, a turpentine mill, three churches, a few general stores, and some schools.

Background of the Massacre

During the 19th century, the whites would often try to establish white supremacy, by lynching black men. This was often done on the grounds of accusing the blacks of attacking or raping white women. In 1919, there was a mass racial violence in several cities in the north due to the competition for jobs as well as place. During the 19th and 20th century, Florida along with other southern states passed various laws and constitutions to disfranchise the blacks, thereby creating barriers in their voting registrations. This also led to their banishment in trials, legislature, local government, or any law enforcement. Additionally, Florida also passed the Jim Crow laws for separate public and transport facilities for the blacks and whites.

Lynching of the blacks had become very common. White mob action would frequently occur in Florida, and could not be controlled by the local law enforcement. Moreover, the membership of Ku Klux Klan, a nationwide organization against the blacks, was also growing. Elected officials in Florida were proving inefficient in easing the racial tension. In 1920, a few white men abducted four black men from a local jail and lynched them after accusing them of raping a white woman. The same year, two white election officials were shot in Ocoee, in a dispute over voting rights. As a result, the black community of Ocoee was completely destroyed by a white mob, causing over 30 deaths and destruction of 25 homes, 2 churches, and a Masonic Lodge. All this laid the foundation of the Rosewood Massacre.b

The carrier family home was burned to the ground by White Klansmen during this horrific stand-off 1923, during 'The Rosewood Massacre"

Residue of one of the houses burned to the ground during "The Rosewood Massacre" 1923

A Chronology of Events

August 5, 1920 – Four black men in Macclenny are removed from the local jail and lynched, for being accused of raping a white woman.

November 2, 1920 – Two whites and five blacks are killed in Ocoee in a dispute over voting rights. The complete black community of Ocoee is destroyed, along with 25 homes, 2 churches, and a Masonic Lodge.

February 12, 1921 – Another black man is lynched in Wauchula for an alleged attack on a white woman.

December 9, 1922 – A black man in Perry is burned for an alleged murder of a white school teacher. Another Masonic Lodge, a black church, a school, and a meeting hall are burned.

December 31, 1922 – A large Ku Klux Klan Parade is held in Gainesville on New Year's Eve.

January 1, 1923 – Fannie Taylor files a report claiming she was sexually assaulted by a black man, early in the morning.

By the afternoon, Aaron Carrier has been comprehended by a posse, and is spirited out of the area by Sheriff Walker.

Late that afternoon, a black man named Sam Carter is killed by the posse.

January 2, 1923 – Armed white forces begin gathering in Sumner.

January 4, 1923 – Late that evening, white vigilantes attack the Carrier house. Several white men are wounded and killed in the attacks. A black woman named Sarah Carrier is killed in the Carrier house. Others inside the house are also killed or wounded.

All the black residents from Rosewood flee to swamps.

Another black church and numerous unprotected homes are burned down.

January 5, 1923 – Approximately 200 – 300 whites from surrounding areas approach Rosewood.

Governor Cary Hardee receives a telegram by Sheriff Walker saying that he fears "no further disorder."

James Carrier is brutally shot, after being forced to dig his own grave.
January 6, 1923 – Refugees approach Gainesville.

January 7, 1923 – A mob of 100 – 150 whites return to Rosewood, and burn all the remaining buildings.
February 11, 1923 – An official meeting of the Grand Jury is held in Bronson for the investigation of Rosewood riot.
February 15, 1923 – The Grand Jury declares to have found insufficient evidence to prosecute any of the accused.

The 1923 Rosewood Massacre

▶ On January 1, 1923, a white woman named Fannie Coleman Taylor from Sumner, Florida, reported that she had been assaulted by a black man early that morning. However, Taylor's laundress, Sarah Carrier, a black woman from Rosewood, who was present in the house that morning claimed that the man was in fact Taylor's white lover. According to her, the white man had assaulted Taylor, after they had a fight. In search of the victim, James Taylor, Fannie's husband summoned a posse and ordered a bunch of tracking dogs. The news of the assault spread in the neighboring communities over January 2nd and 3rd. The white locals were outraged at the thought of a black man abusing a white woman, since they were forbidden from even looking at them. A group of white vigilantes had arrived in Rosewood by January 4.

▶ At the same time, a Ku Klux Klan rally had been held in Gainesville, in opposition of justice for the blacks. James Taylor reported the incident to the KKK members and summoned help from them as well. This meant that a group of 500 Klansmen, determined and outraged, were now headed towards Sumner, at the appeal of James Taylor. Soon after their arrival, they spread out in the woods behind the Taylor residency in search of a suspect. Hours later, a black man named Jesse Hunter, who had allegedly escaped from a convict road gang, was suspected of the crime. No proof of his escape was ever provided though. A few hours later, a black man named Sam Carter, a local blacksmith, was tortured into admitting that he had helped Carter escape. He was alleged to have admitted of doing so. He was, therefore, forced by the posse to show them where he had last seen Hunter. When there was no trace of Hunter, the mob got infuriated. They tortured Sam for several hours, after which they riddled his body with bullets before hanging him from a tree.

▶ The posse continued to search for Hunter in Rosewood, during which one of the tracking dogs led them to Aaron Carrier, who was Carter's cousin and Sarah

Carrier's nephew. The posse dragged Aaron outside his house, tied his neck to a car, and dragged him all the way from Rosewood to Sumner. They tortured him for hours, hitting him, kicking him, and beating him with guns. They planned to shoot him after he fell unconscious, but Sheriff Walker intervened, saying he would finish him later. This saved Carrier's life, even though he was held in jail for several months after the incident.

Rosewood, Florida newspaper,

▶ On January 4, the gathered posse attacked the Carrier house, in which about 15 to 25 blacks had taken refuge. The blacks fought back, thereby wounding two white men. Sarah Carrier was shot in the head during this attack. After shooting for several hours, the posse finally stopped after they ran out of ammunition. As they left Rosewood, they burned down several houses and black churches. On January 5, Sarah Carrier's son, James returned to Rosewood from the swamps. He asked a saw mill supervisor for refuge. However, the mob found him and brutally shot him, after asking him to dig his own grave.

Rosewood, Florida County Sheriff Robert Elias Walker organized a posse of over 500 white townsmen most of them Klansmen to hunt down Jesse Hunter.

▶ As the news of blacks attacking the whites spread around, up to 300 angry white men from Gainesville, Starke, and Perry had gathered in Levy County by January 6. Over the next two days, they burned down the remaining property in Rosewood. All the residents of Rosewood had fled by the time. The town was completely abandoned, and no one ever returned. The survivors even changed their names, fearing they would be tracked down.

No one was ever arrested for the murders committed in Rosewood. An all-white grand jury was set up in Levy County during February 1923 for investigating the matter. However, the case was closed on account of insufficient evidence to make any indictments.*(Ref Historyplex/ 1923 Rosewood Massacre: A Harrowing story of violence and racism*)

The Tulsa Oklahoma Massacre on Black Wall Street 1921

Before the <u>Tulsa Race Massacre</u> where the city's black district of Greenwood was attacked by a white mob, resulting in two days of bloodshed and destruction, the area had been considered one of the most affluent African American communities in the United States for the early part of the 20th century. The massacre, which began on May 31, 1921 and left hundreds of black residents dead and 1,000 houses destroyed, often overshadows the history of the venerable black enclave itself. Greenwood District, with a population of 10,000 at the time, had thrived as the epicenter of African American business and culture, particularly on bustling Greenwood Avenue, commonly known as Black Wall Street.

Developed on Indian Territory

Founded in 1906, Greenwood was developed on <u>Indian Territory</u>, the vast area where Native American tribes had been forced to relocate, which encompasses much of modern-day Eastern Oklahoma. Some African Americans who had been former slaves of the tribes, and subsequently integrated into tribal communities, acquired allotted land in Greenwood through the Dawes Act, a U.S. law that gave land to individual Native Americans. And many black sharecroppers fleeing racial oppression relocated to the region as well, in search of a better life post-Civil War.

<u>Prior to the 1921 Massacre there were a reported more than 600 Black owned businesses</u>.

The Greenwood Community in the 1900's was a self-contained Black owned community that boasted over 600 Black only businesses and more than 10,000 Black residents.

"Oklahoma begins to be promoted as a safe haven for African Americans who start to come particularly post emancipation to Indian Territory," says Michelle Place, executive director of the Tulsa Historical Society and Museum. The largest number of black townships after the Civil War were located in Oklahoma. Between 1865 and 1920, African Americans founded more than 50 black townships in the state. O.W. Gurley, a wealthy black landowner, purchased 40 acres of land in Tulsa, naming it Greenwood after the town in Mississippi.

"Gurley is credited with having the first black business in Greenwood in 1906," says Hannibal Johnson, author of *Black Wall Street: From Riot to Renaissance in Tulsa's Historic Greenwood District*. "He had a vision to create something for black people by black people."

Gurley started with a boarding house for African Americans. Then word began to spread about opportunities for blacks in Greenwood and they flocked to the district.

"O.W. Gurley would actually loan money to people who wanted to start a business," says Kristi Williams, vice chair of the African American Affairs Commission in Tulsa. "They actually had a system where someone who wanted to own a business could get help in doing that."

Other prominent black entrepreneurs followed suit. J.B. Stradford, born into slavery in Kentucky, later becoming a lawyer and activist, moved to Greenwood in 1898. He built a 55-room luxury hotel bearing his name, the largest black-owned hotel in the country. An outspoken businessman, Stradford believed that blacks had a better chance of economic progress if they pooled their resources.

In a time when the entire state of Oklahoma had only two airports, six Black families owned their own planes. The average income for a Black family was well over what minimum wage is today. Dr. Simon Berry, who owned the bus system in Tulsa, recalls that in 1910 his average income was around $500 a day, according to reports from *sfbayview.com*A.J. Smitherman, a publisher whose family moved to Indian Territory in the 1890s, founded the *Tulsa Star*, a black newspaper headquartered in Greenwood that became instrumental in establishing the district's socially-conscious mindset. The newspaper regularly informed African Americans about their legal rights and any court rulings or legislation that were beneficial or harmful to their community.

Demands for equal rights were an ongoing mission for blacks in Tulsa despite Jim Crow oppression. Greenwood itself had a railway track running through it that separated the black and white populations. Consequently, Gurley and Stradford's vision of having a self-contained and self-reliant black economy came to be not only by desire but by logistics.

"As a practical matter they had no choice as to where to locate their businesses," said Johnson. "Tulsa was rigidly segregated, and Oklahoma became increasingly racist after statehood."

On Greenwood Avenue, there were luxury shops, restaurants, grocery stores, hotels, jewelry and clothing stories, movie theaters, barbershops and salons, a library, pool halls, nightclubs and offices for doctors, lawyers and dentists. Greenwood also had its own school system, post office, a savings and loan bank, hospital, and bus and taxi service.Greenwood was home to far less affluent African Americans as well. A significant number still worked in menial jobs, such as janitors, dishwashers, porters, and domestics. The money they earned outside of Greenwood was spent within the district.

"It is said within Greenwood every dollar would change hands 19 times before it left the community," said Place.

The Intersection of Greenwood ave and Archer St. of Greenwood before the
Tulsa race riot massacre of 1921

Tulsa Oklahoma, Black Wall Street before the Massacre of 1921

Money Stayed Inside the Community

The dollar circulated 36 to 100 times in this tight-knit community, according to *sfbayview.com.* A single dollar might have stayed in Tulsa for almost a year before leaving the Black community. Comparatively in modern times, a dollar can circulate in Asian communities for a month, Jewish communities for 20 days and white communities for 17, but it leaves the modern-day Black community in six hours, according to reports from the NAACP.

The Greenwood Community , Black Wall street boasted itself of over 600 Black owned businesses, 21 churches, 30 grocery stores, 2 movie theaters, 6 private airplanes, a hospital

Banks, schools, 21 restaurants, libraries, law offices, even a Black owned bus system.

Black Wall Street, Tulsa Oklahoma 1920's

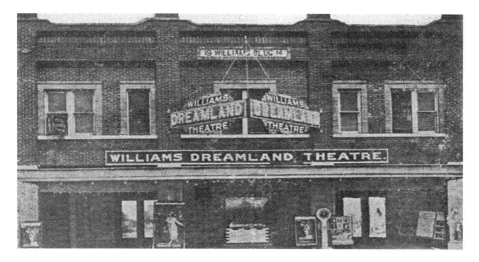

The Williams Dreamland theatre one of two Black owned movie theatres, Tulsa OK

(Tulsa Oklahoma Massacre cont)

Before the Massacre of 1921 Black Businesses thrived in the Black Community of Black Wall Street.

The Greenwood Community was founded by OW Gurley & JB Stradford

O.W. Gurley one of the two founders of Black Wall Street

1. O.W. Gurley was a wealthy Black landowner, born to former enslaved Africans, who traveled the United States to take part in the Oklahoma Land Grab of 1889.
2. The young businessman resigned from a presidential appointment under then-president Grover Cleveland to venture out and found his own town.
3. In 1906, Gurley moved to Tulsa, Oklahoma where he bought 40 acres of land that was only allowed to be sold to Black folks.
4. One of Gurley's first businesses was a rooming house which was built along a dusty trail near the railroad tracks. This road would later become Greenwood Ave. of the legendary Black Wall Street.
5. Adding to the rooming house, Gurley went on to build three two-story buildings and five residential homes. He also purchased an 80-acre farm in nearby Rogers County.
6. The entrepreneur later founded a church, today known as Vernon AME Church.

7. By 1913, more businesses began springing up in Gurley's Greenwood district, including hotels, law and doctor's offices, cafes, pharmacies, barbershops, movie theaters and hair salons. Eventually, there were hundreds of businesses, all were Black-owned and operated.

8. Greenwood's unpaved roads served as Tulsa's racial division lines and African-Americans flocked to the thriving city to escape racial prejudice elsewhere.

9. After years of economic success in the thriving Black "enclave," the entrepreneur lost all he had built after an angry white mob attacked and set fire to the Greenwood district, burning everything to the ground. He lost an estimated $200,000 in the 1921 race war.

10. It was rumored that Gurley had been lynched by a white mob in the race war, but the memoirs of fellow Greenwood pioneer, B.C. Franklin indicate that he exiled himself to California where he later died. *(Ref.Atlanta Blackstar)*

Some of the pioneers of Greenwood, including O.W. Gurley (bottom left).

J.B Stradford

While growing up in the 1950's and 60's in America we, as Black young men and women, were always told that in order to make it in this country we had to be twice as good as the European Americans. Equal opportunity existed only within the framework of that European American community, and we certainly were not allowed inside. If our plight was difficult in the 60's, you can imagine how difficult it was for Blacks living at the turn of the century, and had been out of slavery for less than fifty years. Not only did they have to be twice as good but at least ten times as good just to succeed, and had to be geniuses to build successful businesses. One of those geniuses was John B. Stradford, the richest Black man on Black Wall Street in 1921. His luxurious 54 room Stradford Hotel, located on the famous Greenwood Avenue, was evidence of his brilliance as a businessman. The Stradford Hotel, trimmed in press brick above the windows and stone slabs below, was considered the finest Black owned hotel in the country and even rivaled some of the white owned hotels in Oklahoma. Gorgeous chandeliers hung from the ceilings in the lobby and in the banquet room. The hotel had a pool room for the enjoyment of the guests, a dining hall for the eating pleasure of the guests and a salon for the relaxation of the guests. It was first class all the way. According to Stradford, his structure matched the Hotel Tulsa, "the finest building in the southwest." He also owned fifteen rental houses and an apartment building.

Stradford, the son of an escaped slave Julius Caesar Stradford, received his law degree from Oberlin College in Ohio and migrated to Tulsa, Oklahoma in 1899. He, along with another businessman, O. W. Gurley, set their sights on building a community that would bring tremendous pride to all that lived there. Stradford believed that Blacks in 1921, had the best chance for success in a racist country if they pooled their resources, worked together and supported one another's businesses. Spending within their own community would create self-sufficiency and allow them to achieve some independence. His genius was so timely and his strategy so successful in building an independent commercial business sector along Greenwood Avenue, that when Booker T. Washington visited there, he named it "Negro Wall Street," which has now been changed to Black Wall Street.

The Stradford Hotel

The Stradford Hotel was considered to be the largest Black owned hotel in the U.S

(Ref The writer Fred, The Genius of J.B. Stradford Black Wall Street Entrepreneur)

The 54-room hotel was reportedly the largest black-owned and -operated hotel in America, and it featured a dining hall, gambling hall, saloon and regular Jazz performances for the neighborhood's residents. Forbes notes that Stradford's hotel, boosted by Greenwood's rising success, would eventually be valued at roughly $75,000 (or over $1 million in today's dollars) before it was destroyed in the violence of 1921.

Gurley himself also built a rooming house, multiple rental properties and his own hotel. He also ownd a Masonic Lodge and a successful grocery store, which he supplied with produce from his nearby 80-acre farm. According to Forbes, as Greenwood's population grew, Gurley's fortune was ultimately worth roughly $200,000, equivalent to $2.7 million today. Other prominent Black business-owners in the area included John and Loula Williams, who owned a candy shop and built the neighborhood's Dreamland Theater, a 750-seat movie theater. There was also Andrew Smitherman, a lawyer who also founded and ran the Tulsa Star, one of the area's most prominent Black-owned newspapers.

However, while Greenwood's "Black Wall Street" was a self-sustaining enclave for Tulsa's Black community, it was also only blocks away from predominantly white neighborhoods that remained unwelcoming to their Black neighbors. What's more, racist violence was on the rise in the U.S. at the time. Just two years before the Tulsa Massacre, the nation endured the Red Summer of 1919, when at least 25 riots and incidents of mob violence erupted in major cities across the U.S., killing hundreds of people, most of whom were Black.

Those pre-existing racial tensions set the stage for a bloody day of racist violence that erupted over a nearly 24-hour period, ending June 1, 1921, after an armed white mob descended on the Greenwood District.

The mob attacked black residents and businesses in the neighborhood, leaving 35 city blocks "in charred ruins," according to the Tulsa Historical Society. In the skirmishes, as many as 300 people (mostly Black) were killed and hundreds more were injured, while thousands of Tulsa's black residents lost their homes and businesses.

The violence had been sparked by an incident in the preceding days involving a young African-American shoe-shiner named Dick Rowland, who rode in an elevator operated by a young white woman named Sarah Page. While reports of exactly what happened in the elevator vary, it is widely believed that Rowland accidentally came into contact with Page (perhaps stepping on her foot, or tripping and falling into her, according to different reports), causing her to scream.

One witness who heard the scream called the police, who eventuallyarrested Rowland on May 31. Meanwhile, after a Tulsa Tribune newspaper article falsely claimed that Rowland had assaulted Page, rumors about the incident ran wildly and some accounts even falsely claimed he had raped the woman, according to The New York Times. (Local law enforcement later admonished the Tribune for publishing an "untrue account" that helped to incite the violence, according to the Tulsa World.)

Tulsa's Black residents, fearing that Rowland would be lynched by an angry mob (a horrifically regular occurrence that's estimated to have happened thousands of times in the U.S. during the Jim Crow Era) after he received threats on his life, gathered in front of the city's courthouse where he was being held. A confrontation broke out between black and white groups at the courthouse, both of which were armed, resulting in shots being fired.

After that initial skirmish, Black residents retreated to the Greenwood District, while groups of white vigilantes reportedly spread throughout Tulsa attacking any Black people they encountered, according to the Oklahoma Historical Society. On the morning of June 1, a mob of over a thousand white people overran the affluent Black neighborhood, attacking and shooting residents.

The white mob looted and burned most of the neighborhood, firing on residents who tried to defend themselves but were outgunned by the attackers, some of whom reportedly had machine guns, surviving eyewitnesses later reported. Some survivors even said that the attackers flew over the area in private airplanes, from which they shot at Black residents and dropped firebombs on buildings.

1921 Tulsa Massacre, white Americans burned and destroyed one of the richest Black communities in history killing more than 300 people.

The Oklahoma Historical Society reports that the violence trailed off later in the morning, upon the arrival of troops from the National Guard, though much of the neighborhood was already in ruins by that point. However, other reports suggest that the National Guard and the Tulsa police arrested Black residents instead of their attackers, and that some troops even joined in the attack, according to The New York Times.

In the end, more than 1,200 homes were reportedly burned, leaving most of the Greenwood District's 10,000 residents homeless. Over 6,000 of them were rounded up into internment camps by the local government and forced to live in tents, in some cases for months after the massacre.

The Greenwood District was eventually rebuilt by Black residents who refused to leave the city, starting immediately after the massacre, with hundreds of structures rebuilt by the end of 1921. By 1925, Greenwood hosted the annual conference of Booker T. Washington's National Negro Business League and, by 1942, the neighborhood boasted more than 200 Black-owned businesses, according to a report from the state's 1921 Tulsa Race Riot Centennial Commission.

Still, many of the neighborhood's surviving Black residents never fully recovered the wealth that was lost amid the looting and destruction.

"For years, black women would see white women walking down the street in their jewelry and snatch it off," John W. Franklin of the National Museum of African American History and Culture said in 2016.

1921 The Tulsa Oklahoma Massacre of Greenwood

(Tulsa Oklahoma Massacre cont)

As for individual entrepreneurs, Gurley and Stradford reportedly lost their fortunes in the violence and destruction, and both left Tulsa. Stradford moved to Chicago, where he set up a successful law practice. Gurley moved to Los Angeles, where little is known of what he did before he died in 1935.

Smitherman's newspaper press, business and home were all destroyed in the massacre. He left Tulsa after, fleeing to Massachusetts while reportedly facing some blame from Tulsa authorities for inciting the violence because his newspaper advocated for Black Americans to arm themselves and stand up for their rights.

The Dreamland Theater was rebuilt by the community after the massacre, but the theater and many of the rebuilt neighborhood's businesses eventually shut down a few decades later

An actual picture taken during the Tulsa massacre of June 1921, 'Running Negroes Out Of Tulsa"

The aftermath of the riot forced many Blacks into sleeping in outdoor tents, circa 1921

The aftermath of the bombing of some areas of the Tulsa Riots, circa 1921

(Tulsa Oklahoma Massacre cont.)

The devastation of the Tulsa Massacre, 1921

The destruction of the Dreamland Theatre, which once had 750 seats

Mississippi River Massacre Of Black Union Soldiers 1864

Confederate massacre of Black union soldiers after they surrendered at Fort Pillow, April 12th 1864

April 12 is the 154th anniversary of the Civil War battle and massacre at Fort Pillow, located on the Mississippi River near Henning, Tennessee. It was a strategic location, held by United States (Union) forces just north of Memphis and controlling river access to and from St. Louis and the Ohio River Valley. On April 16, 1864, the *New York Times* reported that rebel forces under the command of General Nathan Bedford Forrest, after twice using a "flag of truce" to maneuver prior to attack, overwhelmed defenders. After taking the fort, "the Confederates commenced an indiscriminate butchery of the whites and blacks, including those of both colors who had been previously wounded." Black women and children in the fort were also slaughtered. "Out of the garrison of six hundred, only two hundred remained alive." In the same issue, the *Times* published an account of events from a "correspondent of the Union, who was on board the steamer *Platte Valley* at Fort Pillow." This correspondent "gives even a more appalling description of the fiendishness of the rebels."

"On the morning after the battle the rebels went over the field, and shot the negroes who had not died from their wounds . . . . Many of those who had escaped from the works and hospital, who desired to be treated as prisoners of war, as the rebels said, were ordered to fall into line, and when they had formed, were inhumanly shot down. Of 350 colored troops not more than 56 escaped the massacre, and not one officer that commanded them survives."

The Black soldiers who were butchered in cold blood by the Confederate troops were regularly enlisted in the Union army, were in full uniform, and were defending the United States flag.

The Black soldiers who were butchered in cold blood by the Confederate troops were regularly enlisted in the Union army, were in full uniform, and were defending the United States flag.General James Ronald Chalmers explained to the *Times* correspondent that the Confederate troops were following orders. It was official policy to kill wounded Black Union soldiers and anyone who surrendered, as well as White officers who served with Black troops.

In battle dispatches, General Forrest wrote, "The river was dyed with the blood of the slaughtered for two hundred yards. The approximate loss was upward of five hundred killed, but few of the officers escaping. My loss was about twenty killed. It is hoped that these facts will demonstrate to the Northern people that negro soldiers cannot cope with Southerners." In response to the massacre, Congress passed a joint resolution demanding an official inquiry, Secretary of War Edwin Stanton initiated a military investigation, and Abraham Lincoln ordered General Benjamin Butler, who was negotiating prisoner exchanges with the Confederacy, to demand that captured Black soldiers be treated the same as White soldiers, a demand that Confederate negotiators rejected.

An enraged Lincoln issued a resolution that for every "soldier of the United States killed in violation of the laws of war, a rebel soldier shall be executed," but it was never been implemented.

Black lives mattered, at least publicly, for about a month, and then the incident was forgotten. There was never a federal response even though the massacres did not stop. In July 1864, Confederate forces under the command of General Robert E. Lee at the Battle of the Crater in Virginia massacred Black United States soldiers who were trying to surrender. (*Ref, Alan Singer, historian professor of education at Hofstra University*)

The Massacre in Memphis 1866

**A Massacre in Memphis:
The Bloody Race Riot of 1866**

The Memphis Massacre of 1866 was a series of violent events that occurred from May 1 to 3, 1866 in Memphis, Tennessee. The racial violence was ignited by political, social and racial tensions following the American Civil War, in the early stages of Reconstruction. After a shooting altercation between white policemen and black soldiers recently mustered out of the Union Army, mobs of white civilians and policemen rampaged through black neighborhoods and the houses of freedmen, attacking and killing black men, women and children. Federal troops were sent to quell the violence and peace was restored on the third day. A subsequent report by a joint Congressional Committee detailed the carnage, with blacks suffering most of the injuries and deaths by far: 46 blacks and 2 whites were killed, 75 blacks injured, over 100 black persons robbed, 5 black women raped, and 91 homes, 4 churches and 8 schools burned in the black community. Modern estimates place property losses at over $100,000, suffered mostly by blacks. Many blacks fled the city permanently; by 1870, their population had fallen by one quarter compared to 1865.

The Memphis Massacre 46 Blacks killed, and women raped, 1866

Public attention following the riots and reports of the atrocities, together with the New Orleans riot in July 1866, strengthened the case made by Radical Republicans in U.S. Congress that more had to be done to protect freedmen in the South and grant full rights. The events influenced passage of the Fourteenth Amendment to the United States Constitution to grant full citizenship to freedmen, as well as passage of the Reconstruction Act to establish military districts and oversight in certain states.[5]

Investigation of the riot suggested specific causes related to competition in the working class for housing, work and social space: Irish immigrants and their descendants competed with freedmen in all these categories. The white planters wanted to drive freedmen out of Memphis and back to plantations, to support cotton cultivation with their labor. The violence was a way to enforce white supremacy after the end of slavery.

The Elaine Race Massacre 1919

The Elaine Massacre is the deadliest racial confrontation in Arkansas history and among the bloodiest racial conflicts in the U.S. At least 200 black people were killed by white people over the course of several days in September 1919.

The Elaine Massacre started Sept. 30, 1919, when African American sharecroppers met to discuss better pay for their cotton. During a union meeting, shots were fired, sparking mass killings. Up to 1,000 white people from surrounding Arkansas counties and as far away as Tennessee traveled to Elaine to take part in the massacre. U.S. troops were eventually called in, and the white mob finally dispersed Oct. 2.

Afterward, more than 200 African Americans were put in jail or stockades, where there were reports of torture. A Phillips County grand jury charged 122 African Americans with crimes connected with the massacre, and a jury convicted 12 African American men of murder. The 12 men were sentenced to death but were eventually released after long court battles.

(Ref, Arkansas State archives a division of the dept of Arkansas heritage)

1919

U.S Army troops took Black men prisoners during the massacre 1919

The Elaine Massacre started Sept. 30, 1919, when African American sharecroppers met to discuss better pay for their cotton. During a union meeting, shots were fired, sparking mass killings. Up to 1,000 white people from surrounding Arkansas counties and as far away as Tennessee traveled to Elaine to take part in the massacre. U.S. troops were eventually called in, and the white mob finally dispersed Oct. 2.

Philadelphia Bombing of 1985

The Philadelphia MOVE organization founded by John Africa (Vincent Leaphart) in 1972

The black liberation group MOVE was founded in 1972 by John Africa (born Vincent Leaphart). Living communally in a house in West Philadelphia, members of MOVE all changed their surnames to Africa, shunned modern technology and materialism, and preached support of animal rights, revolution and a return to nature.

Their first conflict with law enforcement occurred in 1978, when police tried to evict them from their house. A firefight erupted, killing one police officer and injuring several more on both sides. Nine members of the group were sentenced to 100 years in prison for the officer's killing. In 1981, the group moved to a row house on Osage Avenue. At their new headquarters, MOVE members boarded up the windows, built a fortified rooftop bunker and broadcasted profanity-laced political lectures with bullhorns at all hours, drawing complaints from neighbors. Members continued to rack up violations from contempt of court to illegal possession of firearms, to the point where they were considered a terrorist organization by the mayor and police commissioner. On the morning of May 13, 1985, the police moved on the house.

Arriving with arrest warrants for four residents of the house, the police ordered them to come out peacefully. Before long, shooting began. In response to gunfire from inside the house, more than 500 police officers discharged over 10,000 rounds of ammunition in 90 minutes. The house was hit with high-pressure firehoses and tear gas, but MOVE did not surrender.

Despite pleas for deescalation to the mayor from City Council President Joseph Coleman and State Senator Hardy Williams, Police Commissioner Gregore Sambor gave the order to bomb the house.

A helicopter was ordered to drop several bombs on Black residents in the Philadelphia MOVE massacre.

MOVE is short for "The Movement," and it's largely unclear when it began; however, some people have reported remembering the group as far back as 1968. Its founder and leader was John Africa, a man born Vincent Leaphart, who was a handyman for a housing cooperative at 33rd and Powelton in Powelton Village.

Donald Glassey was a Penn grad student who had strong beliefs about the social rights of the poor. After he met Africa, he apparently transcribed 800 pages of Africa's ideas into a document that became the guidelines and the backbone of what MOVE stood for, including everything that is "unnatural" and man-made, according to the book *The MOVE Crisis in Philadelphia: Extremist Groups and Conflict Resolution*.

MOVE wanted to stop man's system from imposing on life, and it taught that man-made creations harm water, air, food, soil and pretty much everyone's lives. MOVE started when Africa's friends and family would sit around with him and study that 800 page document — dubbed "The Guideline" — and soon, the group grew to include a former Black Panther, college students, ex-prostitutes, businessmen and nurses. And while the group was predominately black, it accepted members of all races.

By the late 1970s, it was speculated there were 57 active members and more than 50 "supporters," or people who would deliver food and goods to the group.

MOVE movement members 1980's Philadelphia, PA

A lot. Pretty much everything about how they should live their lives. A few highlights:

- All members of MOVE took the last name Africa, which signified that they were all members of the same "family."
- They opposed technology and didn't use machines, electricity, heat or soap.
- Their diet would consist of almost exclusively fruit, vegetables and nuts. Children would be raised on raw meat.
- Children were not sent to public school, but were instead taught based on The Guideline.

- They would at all times be kind to all animals, including birds, bugs and rats. There were consistently more than 50 or 60 dogs living with the people in MOVE.
- Children would wear as little clothing as possible so their skin could not be tainted.

In August 1978, the city had an eviction order for MOVE's Powelton Village home that ordered police to raid the house, get everyone out and bulldoze it. And firefighters basically flushed them from the home. "Deluge tanks were positioned close to the house," Kitty Capparella wrote, "where they discharged columns of water directly into the basement." MOVE members were physically pulled out of the house by police and violently arrested. A massive shootout ensued, and Officer James J. Ramp was killed. (The Ramp Athletic Fields in Holmesburg are named for him.)

MOVE supporter is arrested 1978(courtesy of the Philadelphia Evening via Temple University archives)

Nine members of MOVE were convicted of murder in Ramp's killing, even though MOVE claimed the shot that killed the officer was accidental friendly fire.

Nope. By 1980, MOVE had regrouped in a new location on the 6200 block of Osage Avenue that was owned by John Africa's sister. MOVE's new neighbors, frustrated with a loudspeaker that constantly sent out statements and diatribes, wanted action from the city.

By May of 1985, D.A. Rendell convinced Mayor Wilson Goode that there was evidence for a search warrant that was signed by Common Pleas Judge Lynne Abraham (yes, that one). The neighborhood was evacuated and barricaded by police on May 12 as cops told MOVE to get out. On May 13, 1985, shots rung out and police used tear gas and water cannons to try to force people to leave. Then, a helicopter dropped a bomb on the roof of the home. Eleven bodies, including John Africa's, were found in the rubble. Out of the home, only one adult and one child survived. Fifty-three homes were destroyed and, in total, 61 were razed.

FBI arresting family members of the MOVE movement.

A commission found that Goode and others had acted recklessly in their decision to drop the bomb, but charges were never filed and Goode was re-elected. It's since cost taxpayers upwards of $45 million over the years to rebuild the neighborhood.

Philadelphia Bombing 1985

1985 Philadelphia MOVE bombing, 11 dead bodies, and 60 destroyed homes.

1985 Philadelphia MOVE bombing aftermath.

1985 Philadelphia MOVE bombing aftermath.

The Dylan Roof Church Massacre of 2015

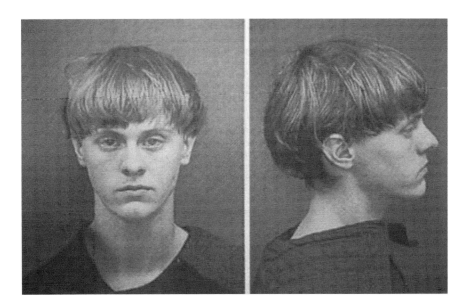

He bought a .45 caliber Glock handgun with money his parents gave him for his 21st birthday and practiced shooting in his South Carolina backyard, taking selfies of himself with Confederate flags. Then, like an increasing number of extremists bent on racial violence, Roof decided to be a lone wolf. He made a list of potential targets, ultimately picking one of the oldest, historically significant black churches in the South where he hoped to kill as many parishioners as possible. He took along 88 hollow-point bullets, symbolizing Heil Hitler, hoping his act would precipitate racial violence. He expected to encounter police, so he saved a few bullets for himself, intending to commit suicide like so many mass killers have done. While his storyline may sound familiar to other premeditated acts of U.S. racial violence, there is one largely new component. He wasn't radicalized by shaving his head bald and joining a neo-Nazi skinhead gang. He didn't attend Ku Klux Klan rallies to soak up hatred around burning crosses. Nor did he attend Aryan Nations churches where the racist religion of Christian Identity is preached. Dylann Storm Roof learned to hate online. Roof used a computer to research racial crimes committed on white victims. He walked away with the convoluted notion that a race war going to be his answer.

Murderer Dylan Roof displays the confederate flag in above picture.

"The event that truly awakened me was the Trayvon Martin case," Roof would write in his 2,500-word manifesto. Martin, a black 17-year-old, was fatally shot in 2012 in Sanford, Fla., by neighborhood watch volunteer George Zimmerman. "It was obvious that Zimmerman was in the right," Roof concluded. "But more importantly this prompted me to type in the words 'black on white crime' into Google, and I have never been the same since that day."

But Roof's online searches quickly took him to one place that proved to be a lynchpin in his own developing views –– the website of the Council of Conservative Citizens, which grew out of a 1950s-era organization that fought school desegregation. The organization opposes race-mixing and also labeled Michael Jackson as an ape while referring to black people as "a retrograde species of humanity." (After the Charleston shooting, the group posted a web site message saying it was "deeply saddened by the ... killing spree.")

Roof's Internet research of black-on-white crimes fueled his radicalization, including anti-

Semitic views. "There were pages upon pages of these brutal black on white murders,"

Roof wrote, saying he "was in disbelief."

"At this moment I realized that something was very wrong. How the news could be blowing

up the Trayvon Martin case while hundreds of these black on white murders got ignored?"

he wrote. He then apparently became convinced that whites in Europe and the United

States were being victimized and force out of jobs by immigrants – the same message

frequently sounded by white nationalists and racist groups rebranded as the Alt-Right.

He posted his views on a website he created, showing a collection of 60 photos suggesting

a fondness for apartheid and the Confederacy, apparently supporting his belief that the

wrong side won the Civil War, trial evidence revealed. He called himself a white

supremacist, a white nationalist and said he supported racist ideas of the Ku Klux Klan and

neo-Nazis, and expressed the view that black people are inferior to whites. "Negroes have

lower IQs, lower impulse control, and higher testosterone levels in general. These three

things alone area recipe for violent behavior." But Roof also was harshly critical of the

cowardice of whites who walked away from issues he apparently believed are destroying

the white race. So the young man from Eastover, near South Carolina's capital, Columbia,

spent six months figuring how he could start a race war, making surveillance trips and a

list of black churches before eventually picking Charleston's Emanuel African Methodist

Episcopal Church -- fondly called "Mother Emanuel."

Actual surveillance camera footage after White Supremist Dylan Roof leaves the Africa Methodist Episcopal Church on the evening of June 17th 2015, after murdering nine innocent Black men and women.

"I have no choice," Roof wrote in his manifesto. "I am not in the position to, alone, go into the ghetto and fight. I chose Charleston because it is most historic city in my state, and at one time had the highest ratio of blacks to Whites in the country." "We have no skinheads, no real KKK, no one doing anything but talking on the Internet," Roof wrote. Well someone has to have the bravery to take it to the real world, and I guess that has to be me."A week before putting his plan into action, Roof stayed briefly at the rural Lexington County, S.C., home of his friend Joseph "Joey" Meek and told him about his intentions. A high school dropout, Meek later was charged with lying to the FBI and concealing a crime. In confessing to those federal crimes, Meek told a judge that he knew in advance of the planned

Massacre, but told no one. He admitted knowing that Roof planned to kill black people at the Charleston church, hoping to "start a race war because nobody else would do it."On the evening of June 17, 2015, Roof drove to Charleston and parked in the Emanuel AME church parking lot. Trial testimony revealed that he sat in his car for several minutes, spending some of that time carefully loading 88 hollow-point bullets –– his symbolic remembrance of "Heil Hitler" –– into eight ammunition magazines that he could quickly use to reload his Glock. After stuffing the semiautomatic handgun and the clips into a fanny pack, Roof entered a unlocked side door of the church and took a seat at a weekly Wednesday night Bible study meeting, spending about 45 minutes with the group, trial testimony indicated. The congregants warmly welcomed the young white man, and handed him a Bible and sheet of scripture verses. He sat down next to the church's pastor, the Rev. Clementa C. Pinckney, who was leading a study of the parable of the sower.

When the study group bowed heads for a final prayer, Roof grabbed his handgun, firing 77 bullets in a blaze of gunfire that echoed through the historic black church. Investigators determined that more than 50 of the bullets struck someone, that each victim was hit at least five times. Roof first shot Rev. Pinckney as others in the Bible study group drove to the floor in fear, seeking cover from the gunfire under round tables where, the prosecutor said, they were summarily executed like animals. The medical examiner concluded that Roof was holding his gun over the victims who were lying still with their arms pulled against them.

The murdered victims of Dylan Roof, innocently shot to death by Roof on July 17 2015, South Carolina

The victims were strangers that Roof did not know: Rev. Pinckney, 41, was the senior

pastor at the church and a South Carolina state senator. Sharonda Coleman-Singleton, 45,

was an assistant pastor at the church and a high school teacher and track coach; Ethel Lee

Lance, 70, was a sexton who had worked at the church for 30 years, and her cousin, Susie

Jackson, 87, was a longtime Emanuel AME Church member who sang in the church

choir; Cynthia Hurd, 54, was a regional branch manager from the Charleston County

Public Library system; Myra Thompson, 59, was a church trustee and a retired teacher and

guidance counselor who was leading Bible study the night of the shooting. And there was

aspiring poet Tywanza Sanders, 26, a 2014 graduate of Allen University. The other victims were Rev. Daniel L. Simmons Sr., 74, a retired pastor who attended Emanuel AME, and Rev.

DePayne Middleton-Doctor, 49, an enrollment counselor at Southern Wesleyan

University's Charleston campus. Two women and an 11-year-old girl survived the shooting

spree. Just 17 hours after the massacre, Roof was arrested without incident after driving

back roads from Charleston to Shelby, N.C. He immediately confessed in a jailhouse

interview with two FBI agents after local police offered him a Burger King

hamburger. "Well yeah, I mean, I just went to that church in Charleston and, uh, I did it,"

Roof responded to investigators in a filmed interview admitted as evidence during the

trial. Pressed for specifics, he added: "Well, I killed them, I guess."

Roof was subsequently indicted by a South Carolina grand jury on 33 hate-related federal

crimes resulting in death. While the federal case moved forward, state murder charges also

were filed and are still pending.

New Orleans Massacre of 1866

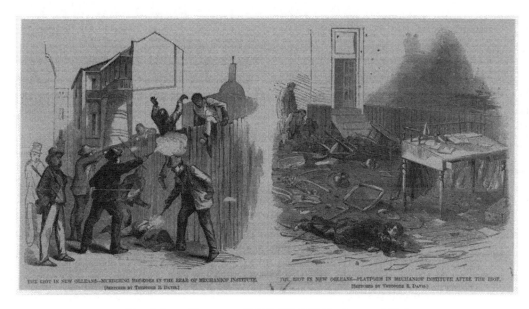

New Orleans Massacre of 1866, 150-200 Blacks were killed

The New Orleans Massacre, also known as the New Orleans Race Riot, occurred on July 30, 1866. While the riot was typical of numerous racial conflicts during Reconstruction, this incident had special significance. It galvanized national opposition to the moderate Reconstruction policies of President Andrew Johnson and ushered in much more sweeping Congressional Reconstruction in 1867. The riot took place outside the Mechanics Institute in New Orleans as black and white delegates attended the Louisiana Constitutional Convention. The Convention had reconvened because the Louisiana state legislature had recently passed the black codes and refused to extend voting rights to black men. Also on May 12, 1866, four years of Union Army imposed martial law ended and Mayor John T. Monroe, who had headed city government before the Civil War, was reinstated as acting mayor. Monroe had been an active supporter of the Confederacy.

As a delegation of 130 black New Orleans residents marched behind the U.S. flag toward the Mechanics Institute, Mayor Monroe organized and led a mob of ex-Confederates, white supremacists, and members of the New Orleans Police Force to the Institute to block their way. The mayor claimed their intent was to put down any unrest that may come from the Convention but the real reason was to prevent the delegates from meeting. As the delegation came to within a couple of blocks of the Institute, shots were fired but the group was allowed to proceed to the meeting hall. Once they reached the Institute the police and white mob members attacked them, beating some of the marchers while others rushed inside the building for safety.

Now the police and mob surrounded the Institute and opened fire on the building, shooting indiscriminately into the windows. Then the mob rushed into the building and began to fire into the crowd of delegates. When the mob ran out of ammunition they were beaten back by the delegates. The mob left the building, regrouped, and returned, breaking down the doors and again firing on the mostly unarmed delegates. As the firing continued some delegates attempted to flee or surrender. Some of those who surrendered, mostly blacks, were killed on the spot. Those who ran were chased as the killing spread over several blocks around the Institute. By this point both the rioters and victims included people who were never at the Institute. African Americans were shot on the street or pulled off of streetcars to be summarily beaten or killed. By the end of the massacre, at least 200 black Union war veterans were killed, including forty delegates at the Convention. Altogether 238 people were killed and 46 were wounded.

The riot's repercussions extended far beyond New Orleans. Northerners angry over the violence helped the Republican Party take control of the U.S. House of Representatives and the U.S. Senate in the Congressional elections of 1866. That Republican controlled Congress subsequently passed the Reconstruction Acts of 1867, a series of measures that called for Army occupation of ten former Confederate states and measures that ensured voting rights for African Americans. Meanwhile martial law was immediately reimposed in New Orleans after the riot and Mayor Monroe and other city officials were forcibly removed from office for their part in the massacre.

(Ref, Black Past Store, April 7th 2011 written by Michael Stolp Smith)

The Slocum Massacre of 1910 Texas

SCORE OF NEGROES ARE SHOT DEAD

RACE RIOT NEAR SLOCUM, TEXAS, RESULTS IN TERRIBLE SLAUGHTER OF BLACKS.

desperate fighting has occurred between bands of armed whites and negroes.

In a race riot at Slocum, Texas, as the result of a cold-blooded murder of a white man by a nego, 20 negroes and three white men were killed.

The Slocum violence was reported (in various degrees of truth) in newspapers across the country at the time.

Slocum Massacre in a Houston newspaper. Image available on the Internet and included in accordance with Title 17 U.S.C. Section 107.

SLOCUM MASSACRE. The Slocum Massacre occurred on July 29, 1910, near the small town of Slocum twelve miles southeast of Palestine in Anderson County. Beginning in the morning of the 29th, white residents of the rural area shot and killed eight unarmed African-American men. The victims, who lived in the same rural neighborhood as their killers, ranged in age from eighteen to seventy. Two others were wounded but survived. Many reasons for the violence have been suggested—ranging from a white man's anger at being told to work with an African American who was placed in charge of a local public road, to a plot by whites to take land from Blacks, to a dispute over an unpaid loan—however, no reason has been clearly established.

Jack Hollie, survivor of the Slocum Massacre. Image available on the Internet and included in accordance with Title 17 U.S.C. Section 107.

State and national newspapers quickly printed accounts of the violence near Slocum and often exaggerated the numbers of Whites in the mob and the numbers of Blacks killed. Anderson County Sheriff William H. Black was quoted as saying: "There was just a hot-headed gang hunting them down and killing them.They were just hunting the negroes down like sheep." Governor Thomas Campbell responded by sending Texas Rangers and state militia into the area to restore order. Eleven local whites soon were arrested, and District Judge Benjamin H. Gardner empanelled a grand jury within a week. On August 17, the grand jury indicted seven men for murder. Their cases were moved to Harris County on a change of venue but eventually were dropped without being prosecuted. Five of the

Indicted men remained in jail until May 1911 because Judge Gardner denied them bail until he was ordered to act by the Texas Court of Criminal Appeals. In the aftermath of the massacre, some African Americans left Anderson County and never returned. Sixteen-year-old Wilustus "Lusk" Holley (often spelled Hollie or Holly), for example, having seen the murder of his older brother Alex and escaping with his own life only by playing dead after being shot, moved to Fort Worth. Others, however, including Reagan and Marshall Holley, older brothers of Alex and "Lusk," lived out their lives in Anderson County. Overall, the African-American population in the Slocum area, while not matching the rate of growth for whites, increased slightly between 1910 and 1920.

Slocum Massacre Historical Marker. Image available on the Internet and included in accordance with Title 17 U.S.C. Section 107.

(Slocum Massacre)

The murders of July 1910, although especially horrible, were but one event in a long train of race-based violence in East Texas during the first half of the twentieth century. Soon the story faded into a past many wanted to forget or ignore. Eventually, however, in 2011, the Eighty-second Texas Legislature adopted a resolution acknowledging the Slocum Massacre, and in 2015 the Texas Historical Commission approved the erection of a historical marker at the site.

Slocum Massacre in a Houston newspaper. Image available on the Internet and included in accordance with Title 17 U.S.C. Section 107.

The Wrightsville Massacre of 1959

1959

On May 5, 1959, a fire broke out in the boys' dormitory at the Arkansas Negro Boys Industrial School in Wrightsville. The "school" was actually a juvenile detention center holding 69 children whose low-level crimes ranged from petty theft to truancy. As the fire spread into the dormitory, the boys inside couldn't get out because the doors were padlocked on the outside. Forty-eight children managed to escape by prying open windows, but the rest perished in the blaze. Their bodies were so badly burned they were unrecognizable.

Fourteen of the children were buried in an unmarked mass grave at the Haven of Rest Cemetery. There was no marker escape by prying open windows, but the rest perished in the blaze. Their bodies were so badly burned they were unrecognizable.

Fourteen of the children were buried in an unmarked mass grave at the Haven of Rest Cemetery. *(Reference Arkansas State Archives*)

1956

The Arkansas Gazette March 6th 1956

The events of that night have been a mystery and are still unknown by many, but not Frank Lawrence who was one of the boys in the dorm that night.

"It was a carefully calculated murder that involved 21 boys but was designed to kill 69 that were housed inside of this dormitory," Lawrence told <u>abc7</u>.
Lawrence dedicated his life to uncovering the truth about what actually happened on that fateful night which he refers to as the "secret holocaust".

THE
WRIGHTSVILLE 21

JOHN DANIEL- 16	ROY HEGWOOD- 15
CECIL PRESTON- 17	FRANK BARNES- 15
JOHNNY TILLISON- 16	LINDSEY CROSS- 15
O.F. MEADOWS- 15	CHARLES THOMAS- 15
HENRY DANIELS- 15	AMOS GYCE-16
EDWARD TOLSTON- 15	JESSE CARPENTER- 16
WILLIE L. WILLIAMS- 15	WILLIE HORNER- 16
JOE C. CRITTENDEN- 16	JOHN A. GEORGE- 15
WILLIE PIGGEE- 15	R.D. BROWN- 16
CHARLES WHITE- 15	CARL THORTON- 15
ROY CHESTER POWELL- 16	

The names of the identified young black youths that were mysteriously murdered

The Memorial stone for "The Wrightsville 21"

Chapter four

More hidden unseen Black art

For centuries Europeans have not only fabricated Black history, but also they have taken great lengths and extreme measures to hide, and cover up our great history. Although you may have some history books that may offer factual evidence of our true histories past. But to understand Black history you have to understand European history in its entirety. During the 1400's which was known as the Renaissance Period, European Italians attempted to pull off one of the most greatest hoaxes known to mankind, and that would be to deceive and cover-up the history of the greatest people that ever walked this earth, and would be the royal bloodline of the original men and women of the past, specifically during the time period when the greatest black history book of all time was written which happens to be the Holy Bible.

In this next chapter you will take a   historical glimpse of unmentioned facts, ancient art that isn't taught or mentioned in educational learning institutions, or modern-day religious facilities. These are Icons, ancient paintings, cathedral sculptures, that your average teacher or professor isn't going to take the time to show you nor explain.

17th Century Russian Orthodox Icon the real image of King David

Black Germany 476 the Black Holy Roman Empire

Julian "the Apostate" Flavius Claudius Julianus Augustus (332–363) aka Julian the Philosopher was Roman Emperor from 361 to 363, and a noted philosopher and writer.

Cameo of Julian the Apostate (Emperor 361-3). Julian attempted to prevent the drift of the Empire towards Christianity, hence his name ' Apostate '. *Bibliothèque Nationale*

Julian the Apostate(Emperor 361-3) noted philosopher and writer

It should be remembered that European Black Christians had no problem with Black Arab Islamists in the Holy lands. The Crusades began only after Albino Turks took control of Islam and the holy lands.

Capture of Jerusalem

The Siege of Jerusalem was part of a military conflict which took place in the year 637 between the Byzantine Empire (The Black Eastern ROMAN Empire) and the Black Arab Caliphate. It began when the Arab army, under the command of Abu Ubaidah, besieged Jerusalem in November 636. After six months, the Patriarch Sophronius (of the Catholic Church) agreed to surrender, on condition that he submits only to the Arab Caliph. In April 637, Caliph Umar traveled to Jerusalem in person to receive the submission of the city. The Patriarch thus surrendered to him. The Muslim conquest of the city solidified Arab control over Palestine.

The First Crusade by Black Europeans occurred in 1096-1099. By then Black Arab Muslims had ruled Jerusalem for 462 years. Clearly Religion was NOT the issue, RACE WAS! As it happens, Black Europe's instincts were correct, the Asian Albinos were a seminal threat, and in time the Albinos would destroy them.

The First Crusade did not commence until after Pope Urban's call at Clermont in 1095. While Christian kingdoms prepared their armies for departure, an ill-equipped mob of peasants under the leadership of the charismatic monk Peter the Hermit attempted to make the crusade on their own. This disorganized event known as the People's Crusade was marked by violence against Jews as the mob made its way across Europe and by its quick defeat at the hands of the Turks.

Although the First Crusade was plagued with hardships ranging from hunger to disease, it nonetheless ended favorably for the Crusaders with the capture of Nicea, Antioch and, most importantly, Jerusalem in 1099.

Carolingian Empire (800–888) is a historiographical term which has been used to refer to the realm of the Franks under the Carolingian dynasty in the Early Middle Ages. This dynasty is seen as the founders of France and Germany, and its beginning date is based on the crowning of Charlemagne, or Charles the Great, and ends with the death of Charles the Fat. Depending on one's perspective, this Empire can be seen as the later history of the Frankish Realm or the early history of France and of the Holy Roman Empire. The term refers to the coronation of Charlemagne by Pope Leo III in 800. Because Charles and his ancestors had been rulers of the Frankish realm earlier (his grandfather Charles Martel had essentially founded the empire during his lifetime), the coronation did not actually constitute a new empire. Most historians prefer to use the term "Frankish Kingdoms" or "Frankish Realm" to refer to the area covering parts of today's Germany and France from the 5th to the 9th century.

Charles V, King of France (1338-80) returns the Sword of the High Constable to Bertrand du Guesclin (c.1320-80) from the 'Histoire de Du Guesclin' after the poem by Cuvelier, early 15th century (vellum)

Charlemagne The Great

Charlemagne Shrine - Commissioned by Henry IV, (1054). Palatine Chapel, UNESCO Site

Casanova

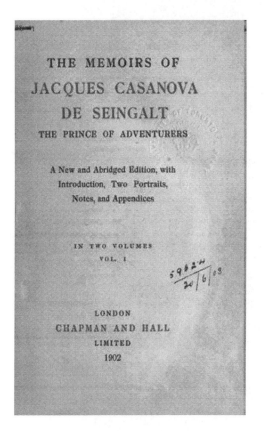

THE MEMOIRS OF
JACQUES CASANOVA
DE SEINGALT

THE PRINCE OF ADVENTURERS

A New and Abridged Edition, with
Introduction, Two Portraits,
Notes, and Appendices

IN TWO VOLUMES
VOL. I

LONDON
CHAPMAN AND HALL
LIMITED
1902

AVENTUROS

PORTRAIT OF CASANOVA BY THE PRINCE DE LIGNE [1]

He would be a very fine man if he was not ugly. He is tall, built like a Hercules, but with an almost African complexion; his eyes are bright, truthful-looking, and intelligent, but they indicate an uneasy susceptibility and a revengeful ferocity; it would seem easier to make him angry than to make him laugh. He seldom laughs, though he makes others do so. He has a way of saying things which reminds one of Harlequin and Figaro.

He knows everything, excepting the things which he prides himself on knowing—such as dancing, the rules of the French language, good taste, and the ways of high society. In the same way, it is only his comedies which are not comic, his philosophical works in which there is no philosophy, all the others are full of it, and of depth, character, piquancy, and originality. He is a mine of science and learning, but wearies one with quotations from Homer and Horace.

His witty sallies have a flavour of Attic salt. He is sensitive and grateful; but when he is displeased, is grumbling, bitter, and altogether detestable. No sum which one could give him would atone for a little joke at his expense. His style is like that of old prefaces—long, diffuse, and heavy—but if he has anything to tell —his adventures, for instance—he tells them so amusingly and dramatically that one is quite carried away. He beats *Gil Blas* or the *Diable Boiteux* in interest. He believes in nothing except what is least worthy of credence, being superstitious on many points. Fortunately, he is high-minded and delicate, for when he says, 'I have sworn to God,' or 'God so wills it,' there is nothing can stop him. He wants everything, and covets everything, and after having possessed everything, he knows how to do without everything.

[1] See de Ligne's *Mémoires et Mélanges historiques et littéraires*, Paris, 1828, vol. iv. p. 291.

Jacques Casanova born April 2nd 1725, Venice Italy, died June 4th, 1798, ecclesiastic, writer, soldier , spy, and diplomatist, chiefly remembered as the prince of Italian adventures and the man known as 'The World's Greatest Lover", he's described in this bio(above)" Memoirs of Jacques Casanova" written about his life in 1902, as someone with " an African complexion"

Holy Roman Empire - Ferdinand I and his son Maximilian II, c.1563

Holy Roman Empire

Elector of Saxony Maurice (1541-1553), 1541 Taler, Annaberg

King David

101. Marble corbel for lintel with figure of King David, c. 1110/c. 1115, Porte Miègeville, Saint-Sernin, Toulouse. (Jean Dieuzaide)

This is a Marble figure of King David outside the Porte Miegeville, (Reference M.F Hearn Romanesque Sculpture) shown in the above sculpture as a black man

Bartholomew and Matthew

Marble Southwest corner pier with shown above of St Bartholomew and the St. Mathew the disciple, c 1100, cloister of Moissac Abbey. (Courtauld Institute-M.F Hearn Romanesque Sculpture), notice the thick lips, and noses

King David

A carving of King David dancing before the Lord, it is thought to have been carved in Egypt in the second or early third century C.E, (Reference, The Illustrated History of the Jewish People by Jane S. Gerber, Oded Irshai)

King Abgarus Receiving the Mandylion, St. Catherine's Monastery, Sinai

ICON of St. Nicholas

Icon of St. Nicholas Mestiya, twelfth Century; state Museum of History and Ethnography of Svaneti Mestiya .

Ancient Painting

Two Archangels, Wings of triptych; Matskhvarishi, second half of the thirteenth century preserved at Matskhvarishi, notice the dark colors of the skin /face , feet and hands.

Ancient painting

Virgin Paraclesis, probably a Greek artist working at Ohrid; St. Sophia, Ohrid thirteenth century; gallery of Icons in the Church of St. Clement, Ohrid, Macedonia.
Notice the dark hands, and facial features

Ancient Painting

The Apostle Matthew, Serbian artist, iconostasis, monastery of Gracanica, mid-sixteenth century; National Museum, Belgrade.

Ancient Painting

Prophet Moses sixteenth century; Monastery of Decani, Serbia

Ancient Icon

Sixteenth century, Monestery of Decani, Serbia, King David

Notice the dark face and hands

Ancient Painting

Sixteenth century; Monastery of Decani, Serbia; the Apostle Andrew

Ancient Painting

Transfiguration, Wallachia , seventeenth century; Museum of Romanian Art,
*Bucharest. * A very dark image of Christ (Yahawahshi) shown above**

Ancient Paintings

Virgin with Child, Monastery of Hurezi, Vilcea district, Wallachia, end of seventeenth century, Museum of the Monastery of Hurezi.

Notice the dark skin and facial features

Ancient Painting

Constantine and Helena, Wallachia , c 1700; Museum of the Monastery of Hurezi.

THESE REMARKABLE WINDOWS AT AUGSBURG CATHEDRAL date from about 1100 and depict the prophets Daniel, Hosea, and Jonah, together with King David. They survive from a cycle of twenty-two figures portraying the Heavenly Jerusalem and remind us that fine windows were not an invention of the French Gothic style.

These remarkable windows at Augsburg Cathedral date from about 1100and depict from left to right, Daniel, Hosea, and Jonah, together with King David.
*(Notice the dark facial features, hands, and feat)

The Assumption Cathedral

(the outside of the Assumption Cathedral) The cathedrals history carries our imagination back into the hoary past. The cathedral of the Assumption built in the 15th century, Kremlin, Moscow.

The Assumption Cathedral

*(The inside of The Assumption Cathedral), the interior of the Assumption Cathedral, vaults and drum of the central dome. Paintings of the ancient prophets, arc angels, Christ and disciples, ** (*Notice the dark facial colors) **

Inside the Assumption Cathedral Dionysius Peter's Ordainment Boarder Scene from the icon Metropolitan Peter with scenes from his life, From The Metropolitan of Russia

The Annunciation Cathedral

(Outside of The Annunciation Cathedral), one of the most popular museum in the Moscow Kremlin, 15th century, its collections of masterpieces of pictorial ancient art including works by Andrei Rubliov.

The Interior of The Annunciation Cathedral

The interior of the Annunciation, the museum boast of a rare ancient icon collection it allows visitors to examine works of 13th century icons from the appearance of Michael The Arc Angel to Joshua the prophet, (the icons shown are all dark colored)*

The Interior of The Annunciation Cathedral

The north and west portals of the Cathedral of the Annunciation through which official processions in state passed, as you can clearly see the top layer of this designed wing has works and carvings of black colored biblical men.

The Annunciation Cathedral

The figures shown above of the Grand Princes of Moscow Dmitry and his son Vasily l.

The interior of the Archangel Michael Cathedral

Fresco showing the images of Russian Grand Princes on the north western pier 17th century. This is the oldest and biggest "portrait gallery" in old Russian pictorial art, compromising of more than fifty full-length figures. 17th century Moscow dynasty.

School of learning, contact Zaaqan at zaaqan1212@yahoo.com

For more information, professional historical lectures, book signings
please contact Frank Zaaqan Jordan zaaqan1212@yahoo.com

Help support your history, Cash app@, $Zaa12

"Never be afraid to learn that which wasn't taught"

We Once Were A Family, The Disappearance Of Black Culture and Soul

This book was written to give a clear understanding and a pictorial history as it pertains to the riches, community ownership of Blacks during the Segregation era of America. Blacks owned hospitals, banks, educational institutions, pharmacies, ect... This book not only shows the greatness of Blacks, but it also proves that Integration (Gentrification), was the beginning of the end for the Black community as we know it.

Available on Amazon.com

The Holiday Hustle, Controlling the Black Mind and Finances

This book details how Cooperate America has systematically set in place a debt credit society, which mainly focuses on the Black and Latino community spending and controlling our Black dollars. Black Americans for over 400 hundred years have celebrated and honored Roman established so-called holidays, these days are pagan, and has little to nothing to do with the bible.

Available on Amazon.com

Uncovering The Evil of Amerikka, What The FDA, Pharmacies, And The CDC Fail To Tell You.

This book has won the 2018 Nat Turner Library Museum Book of The Year Award. The CDC and FDA work hand in hand and continually to approve toxic and in most cases lethal food chemicals into the very food that we consume on a daily basis. Cancer ingredients has been known to be approved by the FDA and CDC to intentionally send patients to get treated, under scientific names these toxic food ingredients go unnoticed in supermarkets we purchase form every day.

Available on Amazon.com

The Greatest Show On Earth
The Destruction of a Chosen Nation

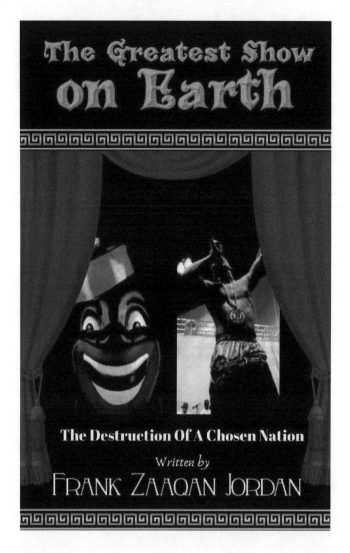

Caucasians have taught and deceived Blacks for centuries how not to love themselves or their own people through what we know today as white supremacy. White Europeans through lies, false history and the media have set a lethal platform for Blacks and Latinos called Christianity, along with self-hate. This book historically details the true history of the greatest people that have ever graced this planet, and their all men and women of color, William Shakespeare, Beethoven, all the prophets and disciples of the ancient world were all Blacks. This award winning, Best-Selling history book will leave you shocked, and enlightened.

Available on Amazon.com

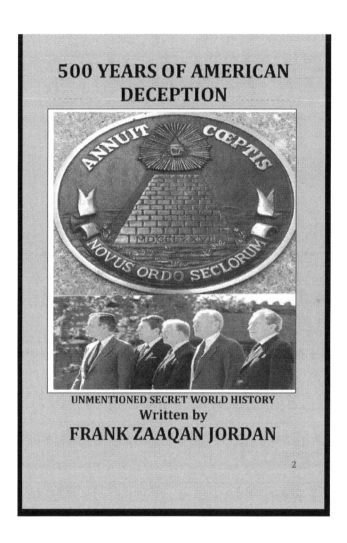

During the 14th Century The Italian Renaissance was one of the most cruel deceptive time periods in the history of man-kind. Famous European painters such as Rembrandt, Leonardo DeVinci along with a host of others were commissioned by the Popes of Rome to attempt to wipe out and "Re-Do" the original Black biblical art, which included the original paintings of all the true biblical prophets, and disciples. This was done over the course of decades, while most people today haven't a clue of why these Popes ordered such an act of man. The truth may shock you.

Not Just A Coincidence, What Pastors, Leaders, and Politicians Fail To Tell You.

The everyday dilemmas that Blacks have faced in America, from slavery, intentional police brutality, being discriminated against, earning low wages, living in unbearable conditions, generation after generation, one can only surmise or be think to themselves, are these just historical mis-haps or can one say these everyday occurrences are "not just a coincidence" This book takes a historical look at the conditions that Blacks and Latinos are faced and challenged with, historically there is an explanation, this is something your school teacher will not teach you.

Available on Amazn.com

Made in the USA
Columbia, SC
29 December 2020